CAN PARLIAMENT SURVIVE?

CAN
PARLIAMENT
SURVIVE ?

by

CHRISTOPHER HOLLIS,

M.P.

"The Socialist régime has given a tremendous impetus to conservative tendencies."—BERTRAND DE JOUVENAL

KENNIKAT PRESS
Port Washington, N. Y./London

CAN PARLIAMENT SURVIVE?

First published in 1949
Reissued in 1971 by Kennikat Press
Library of Congress Catalog Card No: 78-118476
ISBN 0-8046-1225-0

Manufactured by Taylor Publishing Company   Dallas, Texas

CONTENTS

CHAPTER I

FREEDOM IN THE INDUSTRIAL AGE

IT REQUIRES no very profound powers of observation to discover that there is a disease in the modern world, but of the cause of that disease there is less certainty. The two most common diagnoses are that our troubles are due to the war, or wars, and that they are due to poverty, and indeed the greater part of political effort is on the assumption that these are our diseases and that for a remedy to our troubles all that is needed is to banish war and poverty from our lives. But it is clear that both these diagnoses are, if not wholly false, at least inadequate. The war may indeed have aggravated our disease. It obviously has, but it is as obvious that, had a disease not previously existed, there would have been no war.

War is a profound mystery. Man, alone among living beings, kills when it is not necessary for him to kill either for food or for self-defence. There must be some profoundly mysterious force in human affairs which makes it possible to send millions in every quarter of the globe off to kill fellow men whom they have never seen and of whom it can only be pretended that they threaten their way of life in the most indirect and uncertain fashion. It is idle to say that everything was satisfactory until the catastrophe of 1914 or the catastrophe of 1939 upset it. For if there had not been something very wrong with the world already in these years, it would not have blundered into war. It is idle to console ourselves with the absurd superficiality that everyone else was good but that one bad man—the Kaiser or Hitler—or a group of bad men—or one bad nation plunged the world into war. The whole world must have been living under some profound psychological strain. There must have been some mortal madness upon it for it to have admitted such a catastrophe. It is idle, even if it were possible, to seek to put the clock back to 1913, for 1913 would clearly only be once more the prelude to 1914.

It is equally obvious that poverty is not the cause of our disease. That there is poverty in the modern world is true. That poverty, in the sense of men and women not possessing the material necessities to keep them in health— that poverty of such a sort is an evil is certain. That we should do what we can to abolish it, is admitted. But it is equally certain that this is not an especial disease of these last years. It has hung over the whole life of our generation alike in good times and in bad. It has not been the special product of the austerity of to-day nor of the war of yesterday nor of the unemployment of the day before yesterday, and without going into ephemeral controversies whether standards are better or worse in one modern period than in another, the general truth is manifest that there is much less poverty in our life than there was in the lives of our ancestors. Yet they were able to accept their poverty. They did not like it. They would rather have been richer. Sometimes they revolted against it. But it did not cause them to despair. It did not cause them to wish to die. What is the reason why the modern man, endowed with material amenities that to previous ages were either unknown or could only have been found in kings' palaces, sees life as unfaceable and contents himself to complain of his poverty? It is obvious that schemes for increasing productivity, for reorganizing industry or economic systems, however sound and desirable in themselves, are as total remedies intolerably insufficient.

It is quite clear that behind the political and economic problems of the day lies a profound psychological and religious problem, and that it is idle to attempt to solve the former without first solving the latter. Professor Jung in his *Essays on Contemporary Events* sets out his diagnosis of the disease of the modern world. It is this. Throughout all history until a generation or two ago the vast majority of mankind lived in small units and men's natures have been shaped over the generations to meet the needs and loyalties of those small units. Until recently the vast majority of men lived in the village and predominantly in their family units. They rarely, if ever, left their village and its neighbourhood. They accepted a traditional religion. They worked for a lord or an employer, whose name they knew and whom from time to time they saw. So far as they owed a larger loyalty, it was also to a known person—to a king, to whom they gave their loyalty as to the head of a larger family.

It is true, of course, that throughout all history, and in the nineteenth century more commonly than in any previous age, a number broke with their ancestral ties and drifted off into the great metropolitan towns. There some sank beneath the level of their origins. Others rose above it, and it was predominantly from the towns that there came those contributions to thought and methods of production which together make up what we call progress. But society could absorb this progress—or at the least was not asked to progress so rapidly as to fall into catastrophe—because the forces of change in the towns were always balanced by the strong conservative forces of the countryside.

Now all that has altered. A few intellectuals, working in a predominantly stable and conservative society, are an asset to that society. But rootless intellectuals, acting upon a society of rootless proletarians, are a danger. They bring to society's controversies an envy and malice which are unknown among those who have a place in the life in which they live. It is the paradox of the history of class war that so much of its bitterness has come from men who are fighting against the class to which they naturally belong.

We find in our sad age the extremes of disintegration in the deserter and the displaced person, wandering hopelessly over the face of a world in which there is no place to which he can belong. It is one of the great evils of our modern police states, with their passports, their identity cards, their ration cards and controls of engagement, that, if once an unfortunate has put a foot wrong at all, then he is very easily driven down willy-nilly from depth to depth until at last he reaches the final abyss. But it is not only the exceptionally unfortunate who have suffered disintegration. Changes in methods of production incomparably more rapid than were known in any previous age have destroyed the whole conservative balance of society. Family ties have weakened. The force of religion has diminished. The uprooted, who have torn themselves from their ancestral origins, are no longer a minority but in such countries as Britain a majority. The greater number of them work not for a known master but for vast impersonal concerns—the State, it may be, or some gigantic combine or business, ruled by distant men whom they never see and whose very names they often do not know. It is literally impossible for many workers to discover what are the names of those for whom they are working even supposing that they wish to do so. The calamities of life do not come to them, as they did to their grandparents, from blunders of their own or even from the faults of neighbours or of masters whom they can see. They come from vast, anonymous, cyclical forces. They open their papers and read that there is an international crisis about some problem of which they have never previously heard. A few days pass and the crisis perhaps is transformed into war. It is true, of course, that there were wars in previous ages and that the causes of the wars were as incomprehensible to the ordinary man as are those of to-day. But those wars were not totalitarian wars. They did not upset the rhythm of the ordinary man's life as do the modern wars.

Or again even more numbing to the ordinary man than war, of which some explanation is given, even though it be not a true explanation, are the buffets of the trade cycle. Suddenly, for no reason that he can understand, for no reason for which he is in any way responsible, he finds that the market for which he has been working is closed to him and he is unemployed. The ordinary man does not understand why this has happened and it is very doubtful whether the extraordinary man understands either. For, though the pundits are ready enough with an explanation after the calamity has fallen, the ordinary man is quite intelligent enough to notice that the pundits rarely seem able to foretell these calamities before they come, and even after they have come, the explanations of one pundit do not usually agree with those of another.

> Tiny and afraid
> In a world he never made,

he is left to face alone the buffetings of a universe as cruel as it is apparently unmeaning.

> "The shadow of that hideous strength
> Sax myle and more it is of length",

as Mr. C. S. Lewis quotes on the title page of his book of that name from Sir David Lindsay's *Ane Dialog*.

As I came yesterday out of the village post office, I ran into two men who were mending a telephone wire.

"If you ask me, this country's finished", the one was saying.

"If you ask me, the whole bloody world's finished", answered the other.

But why?

It is clear that Man, as he is at present constituted, is not a creature who can feel at home in the modern world, and in his disintegration he is rapidly turning the world into a vast lunatic asylum. He was made for the world of small units and he does not feel that he belongs to the world of large units. Somehow or other we have got to remake Man— to reshape him so that he can become integrated into this new world of the larger units. That is the problem of modern politics and nothing else is its problem. All else is but sound and fury.

By this test many of the most loudly trumpeted of remedies are found not to touch the disease at all.

The historian or the student, for instance, may argue whether another age was happier than ours. It may be that it was, but the demonstration, even if it could be given, is only of academic interest. Even if it be true that we were happier, when we lived our simpler lives in our smaller units, that does not mean that it is now possible for us to go back to those smaller units. There are now forty-five million people on these islands—not ten million. Whether we like industrialism and the machines or not, we cannot escape them. A gospel of "back to the middle ages" is no gospel. We cannot avoid the modern world. We have to find a way of integrating the ordinary man into it.

If the reactionary policy of scrapping all machinery is useless, the equally reactionary policy of returning to the economic system of a hundred years ago is equally useless. The economic system of a hundred years ago was pre-dominantly the system of *laissez-faire*. Of course, in real life we never find perfect examples of any theoretical system, and even in the hey-day of *laissez-faire* there were violations of the principle. The first Factory Acts were passed before the last Corn Laws were repealed. But predominantly the system which Ricardo praised and Marx denounced was a system under which production was financed by private money, looking for a reward in profit; in every industry there were a considerable number of capitalists in competition with one another, and the State as a rule confined itself to the enforcement of contracts and did not otherwise interfere in the workings of industry. To return to that system is a hopeless policy. It is hopeless for two broad reasons. First, in this, as in all reactionary policies, you do not really restore the past. You restore merely one item out of the policy of the past, in whose whole picture it per-haps found a place, and put it into a radically different picture. This Ricardean system may (or may not) have been the best system for industry in the 1850's. The matter is debatable. But in any event the circumstances under which it worked have to-day passed away, and no one has played a larger part in their destruction than have the capitalists themselves. Marx and Ricardo thought of a factory as an independent unit, owned by one or by a very few people. Its owner lived by the factory and himself managed it.

There was genuine competition between factory and factory. It is capitalism, not Socialism, which has over a hundred years brought all that to an end. It is capitalism, which, moved to some extent by greed but more by technological necessity, has substituted for the world of the individual factory the world of the big unit, of combine and of cartel—the world in which ownership is too distant and too indirect for it any longer to be identical with management. It is again capitalism, which by raising the worker's standard of living has made it possible for him to save, so that, from the 1930's onwards, the bulk of the investments in new industry came from people of moderate means investing, as a rule indirectly, through various finance companies. The patter of the platform still speaks of the controlling power of the shareholder. The reality is that the vast majority of those who invest in modern industry neither exercise any control nor wish to exercise any control but invest with the deliberate desire to get a return on their money without being bothered with responsibility. The control is coming to be increasingly exercised by managers, who usually are not shareholders at all, or who hold merely a formal qualifying share.

But the second reason why the cause of Conservatism cannot be defended by a mere clamour for a reaction to the past is an even stronger one. It is most powerfully developed by Professor Schumpeter in his famous defence of capitalism in *Capitalism, Socialism and Democracy*. People sometimes speak as if there were some form of economic organization, which has existed since the beginning of history, as if Socialism was but an eccentricity and all that was required was that society should recover its wits and return to normal. Now there have been in history forms of social organization which were intended to be permanent in a society which intended to be static. Such forms have survived for a long time, and, if they have perished at last, as is the way of all things human, they have perished for reasons that were both unforeseen and undesired. But capitalism never was such a system even in intention. Its whole intention, its whole boast, was that it was a dynamic system, justifying itself by the rapidity with which it was transforming society, and, transforming everything else, it was also inevitable that it should also transform itself. Marx was wrong in many things, but in one thing he was certainly right—in his belief that history consisted of a succession of passing phases, "epochs" as Engels called them. The period of *laissez-faire* was certainly such a phase and it will most certainly not return.

The normal, if there be a normal, is that man is a social animal who finds his fulfilment in a number of organic relationships. Ricardean capitalism was not a conservative creed; it was of its nature a revolutionary and an inconoclastic creed. It destroyed ruthlessly all traditional relationships that stood in its way. It weakened the bonds of family. It proclaimed it as a gospel of progress that man should no longer be tied to his home but should rather be both encouraged and compelled to move both himself and his money over the world in indifference to a constricting patriotism and at the sole call of profit. It remorselessly destroyed the feudal relics. It weakened monarchy and aristocracy and the landed interest.

It destroyed, indeed, all relationships that were not to the interests of the capitalists and preserved only those that were to their interests. Even there the pretence of basing itself upon a psychological principle was a thin one. Its claim was that, if the sole bond between men was the cash nexus, then the price mechanism and the profit motive would cause people to work hard out of self-interest and the consequence of this harsh but healthy discipline would be that idleness would be banished from the land, that enterprise would be rewarded and that as a result more would be produced for everybody than under some softer and more sentimental system.

There was a logic, if a hard logic, in the argument. But, if it be true that men will only work if they are compelled to work by necessity, why should the capitalist system admit inherited wealth? The inheritance of wealth on its own premises must be a great discourager of enterprise. It would be much better, indeed even much kinder, to compel every man to start from nothing. It was the vice of this early capitalism that it destroyed all privileges save those that were to its own convenience. It attacked the family when it was to its own interest to attack it, and it supported it when it was to its interest to support it, and, that being so, it could not defend itself on a moral basis. Now a system which cannot defend itself on a moral basis cannot make any demand on a person's loyalty. It can merely make a pragmatic claim. As long as it can say, "I do not know whether this is a right system or not, but in fact everybody is getting richer under it", there is a case for it, but it has no case against the man who says, "I do not like it." It has no case against the man who says, "It may provide full scope for your initiative but it does not provide scope for mine." If the capitalist can destroy feudal privileges because they interfere with capitalism's freedom of enterprise, then the worker can destroy capitalist privileges because they interfere with the workers' freedom of enterprise.

It is idle to say, "If only the worker would be content with the system as it was, all would be well." First, the worker will not be content with the system as it was, but, second—and far more important—capitalism has in any event destroyed the system as it was, quite apart from anything that the worker may do. The worker at the conveyor belt in the modern giant multiple factory, playing his part in an industry where production is probably largely regulated by agreements between its various capitalists, is himself, for better or for worse, a wholly different being from his grandfather, making something in a small factory for a capitalist who was in genuine competition against his rival capitalists. He is a different being and therefore must have a different system. Whether such a system should be called a new form of capitalism or be called something else is largely a matter of words upon which the wise man will not bother to delay. The important question is what the new system shall be, not what it shall be called. The old Ricardean system has passed away, not because of its follies or its crimes, but because it was of its essence a transitional system. You cannot restore it once it has perished any more than you can restore a fallen dynasty. It is of its essence a bridge from something to something else. To what?

If capitalism is not the solution of our problem, still less is its "Siamese twin",[1] Socialism. There are two quite separate arguments for Socialism, which, though these are often found in the same mouth, are in reality contradictory of one another. On the one hand, there is the apocalyptic argument by which the whole of society is divided into the children of darkness, the bourgeoisie, and the children of light, the workers. There is an irrepressible conflict between them, and Socialism can only be established when good has triumphed over bad and when the wicked capitalists have been expropriated by the virtuous workers. There is quite a different argument according to which for a variety of technical reasons capitalism becomes with the passage of years increasingly irrelevant. It becomes less and less to the interests even of the bourgeois to maintain it. With the growth of large units and indirect methods of investment, ownership and management become increasingly divorced from one another. With heavy taxation and death duties the attractions of personal savings and large fortunes are far less than they used to be. On the other hand social services guarantee to everybody, even if he has no savings of his own, amenities which in a previous age were out of reach of the unmoneyed man. The incentives of industry are less exclusively in monetary form than they used to be. Power is no longer necessarily in the hands of those who have wealth. So for many reasons it is both more difficult to

[1] This central phrase of Mr. Drucker's is often misunderstood. It does not of course mean that there is no difference between capitalism and Socialism. It means, as it says, that they are inseparable—that Socialism may flourish as a criticism of certain excesses of capitalist society but that it provides no remedy for those excesses, and, therefore, if capitalism should perish, the Socialist criticism of it also automatically perishes, being no longer relevant to the real world.

make a large fortune and less worthwhile making it than it used to be in Victorian days, and in such a situation it is possible, if the points are put moderately and persuasively, to persuade the bourgeois that it is really to his interest that there should be a Socialist State and that he will have more power in such a State than in attempting to prop up a dying capitalism. On the other hand, it is, according to this argument, greatly to the interest of the Socialists to attract to their side as many of the bourgeois as possible. They want their numbers because they want their votes, and they want individuals of ability because they want to use that ability. One of the main problems of the Socialist state will be the problem of getting enough brains to run it. Capitalism, whether it was a good or a bad system, at least attracted to it during its years of vigour the ability of society. It is essential that Socialism should annex to its service the ability of the capitalists and of the members of their families, trained naturally to take responsibility.

It is clear enough that these two arguments—the one essentially the argument of such statesmen as Mr. Shinwell and Mr. Aneurin Bevan, the other of Mr. Morrison or Mr. Attlee—are contradictory of one another. Both cannot be true. It may be that neither is true. It is certain that, if the Socialists cannot even make up their minds which of them they think is true, the attempt to pursue two contradictory objectives will infallibly mean that they attain neither.

State Socialism does not solve the problem of the age. It neglects it. To begin with, it takes refuge in a misty generalization that is meaningless. It professes to solve problems by conferring powers on the state—as if there was some person called the state, immaculately conceived and freed from the failings of mortality. But government by the state, of course, only means government by the statesmen and we have to ask what manner of men the statesmen are and how they are to be appointed. They may be better or they may be worse than other men, but they are not fundamentally different. But beyond that, though Socialism, like most of the other words in political controversy, may

mean anything or nothing, Socialism in its usual sense and
as it is to-day being applied in politics is not a remedy but
an aggravation of the disease of our age. If Socialism
merely means that we should do what is in the interests
of society, then obviously we are all Socialists, but the profession does not get us very much further as the whole issue
is *what* is the interest of society. But, if Socialism means
nationalization and the rule of managerial boards, then it
means merely a substitution of bigger units for big units
and has no contribution at all to make to the problem of the
day, which is the discovery of a method of giving to the
ordinary man a real membership in the large units in which
modern conditions compel him to work.

Professor Laski in his *Grammar of Politics* confesses the
bankruptcy of Socialism before this problem. "The mass of
men and women who, at the electoral period, function as
that Demos in whom all power is vested, are very impressive
in their numbers but, alas, in nothing else. They are scarcely
articulate about their wants; and even when they are
articulate they are not trained to judge whether the solutions
suggested are in fact an adequate response to their desires."
We have, he finds, the "basic condition that ultimate power
must be confided to those who have neither time nor desire
to grasp the details of its workings. Their capacity will
be exhausted by the mere effort to live; and the search to
understand life will lead them into complexities they have
rarely the energy, and seldom the leisure, to penetrate.
The context of their lives, which is, for the majority, the
most important, is a private context . . . they set their wills
by the wills of institutions they rarely explore. . . . They
obey the orders of government from inertia; and even their
resistance is too often blind resentment rather than a reasoned
desire to secure an alternative."

If Socialism is no solution, Communism is even less
of a solution. There is little difficulty in picking holes in the
logic of the Marxian thesis, in exposing the crudity of its
psychology, in showing, as the great anarchist, Bakunin,
showed at the time when Marx first enunciated the theory,

that it is idle to expect the classless society to emerge out of the dictatorship of the proletariat. Power of its very nature tends to corrupt, and to expect men to wield the powers of dictatorship and not be corrupted by it, just because they are called Communists, is childish. But Communism is bound to remain powerful and a menace so long as it is only confronted with a negation. Something will always conquer Nothing. You can only conquer an idea with an idea. Goebbels used to jeer at the Allies during the war, saying that they were very certain what they were fighting against but did not seem nearly so clear what they were fighting for. The years since the war—these miserable years of folly— have shown the justice of his jeers. To-day the Communists have annexed his laughter and with an equal justification. If we would repulse Communism, it is not sufficient to fight Communists or to persecute them. We must answer their idea with our idea.

The problem is the problem as set out by Mr. Peter Drucker in his chapter on "A Conservative Approach" in his *Future of Industrial Man*. It is "to prevent centralized bureaucratic despotism by building a genuine local self-government in the industrial sphere". That is the problem, and that alone is the problem in opposition alike to reactionary Socialism, to reactionary capitalism and to romantic dreams of a vanished world. Of course, efficiency is important. We must be careful of utopian schemes which in the name of some ideal freedom rob industry of that measure of discipline and managerial authority which is necessary for efficient production. At the same time, efficiency is not all. We must be equally careful not to allow the claims of a short-term efficiency to refuse expression to the full personality of the worker—a refusal which in the long run would not give us even efficiency. To strike the balance between the claims of order and the claims of liberty is difficult here as elsewhere; yet it is idle to say merely that the solution is difficult. Of course the solution is difficult, but it is also necessary if we are to survive.

It goes without saying that this problem of integration

cannot be solved solely by political and industrial changes. On the contrary, Professor Jung, writing from outside and purely as a psychologist, sees religion as the main agency of the change. In religion alone is there a power strong enough to remake man so that he can be at ease in this new world. For 1,700 years after the birth of Christianity all the controversies of Europe were theological controversies. However unworthy he may at times have been to ask such a question, the only serious question that European man debated was, "What is the mind of Christ?" About that alone he fought. It was the classical economists, and then after them the Marxians, who first attempted to erect a system of conduct to which Christianity was merely irrelevant. The ruins of the attempt now lie patent around us.

Chapter II

THE GROWTH OF PARTY GOVERNMENT

IF WE have defined our aim, then the first question to ask is whether our existing institutions are capable of satisfying that aim. Wise statesmanship will always use traditional and existing institutions, if it can, rather than create new ones. Men obey willingly that to which they are accustomed, where they will only obey a novelty under force.

We live in Britain under a Parliamentary Government, worked on a predominantly two-party system. Since it exists, some Englishmen think of the two-party system as a self-evident truth—think that it somehow stands to reason that on every matter there should be two opinions and neither one nor three and that those who think alike on A, B and C must also, if they are honest men, think alike on D, E and F. This is obviously hardly so. A two-party system, whatever else we may think of it, is certainly an artificial oddity and it is worth while considering how it came to be and why and whether the benefits of it outweigh its evils and absurdities.

The student of history cannot believe that there is any single consecrated, final form of government—whether it be democracy or some other—towards which mankind is inevitably moving. If any of the philosophers have any lesson to teach us about constitutional history, there would appear to be a great deal more truth in the Platonic theory that constitutions move round in a cycle, each form taking its turn and giving place after a time to another, and indeed all forms of government are so manifestly bad and some form of government is so manifestly necessary, that it is not surprising that men should always be acutely conscious of the defects of the particular form from which they are suffering at the moment, should willingly change it for another, only to find that the new form has also its deficiencies. "No one", said Doctor Johnson, "would be of any profession as simply opposed to not being of it, but everyone must do something." And in much the same way every man would rather not have any particular government as opposed to having it, but a nation must have some government.

Yet even the belief in the Platonic cycle, much nearer to the truth as it is than the Macaulayesque or Marxian belief in a straight upward line of continuing progress—"on and on, up and up", as Ramsay MacDonald once put it—is yet only superficially true—at least of modern times. It is true that the changes have been rung throughout all history, between democracy, aristocracy and monarchy, and doubtless will continue to be rung, but we know comparatively little about how a country is governed, if we merely know the name by which the Government calls itself. We know little enough at the best of times, and we know nothing at all at such a time as this, when there is no longer a pretence that such terms as "democracy" or "fascism" are used with any objective, impartial meaning but where they are employed merely as terms of eulogy or of abuse, where a democratic government is a government that one likes and a Fascist government is a government that one does not like, where a Fascist has come to mean little more than a man who prefers the interests of his own country to the interests of the Soviet Union and a worker is a man who supports the ruling Communist class, though he has never done a day's work with his hands in his life. Communism, which was once an economic creed, no longer has, over the short term, any economic meaning at all. The Communists are for the American Loan to-day and against the Loan to-morrow, for the war to-day, against it to-morrow, for it again the day after, with completest opportunism. Communism is simply a gang of people who are in power or a gang of people who want to be in power. It has no more to do with the workers than it has with the man in the moon.

But this is an exceptional evil of our day. It is possible to use terms with responsibility. Yet, obviously such terms, even when so used, obscure the truth—insisted upon by Marx and other thinkers—that every new economic form of society demands a new form of political expression. The old society and the new society may, if you will, both be aristocratic or both be democratic, but the new aristocracy will be a different aristocracy from the old and the new democracy will be a different democracy from the old. Sometimes the change is noted by a violent and overt revolution. At other times an appearance of continuity between old and new is preserved. But it would be a great mistake to imagine that, just because there has been formal continuity and has been no violent overthrow, therefore there has been no change. Indeed the study of the constitutional changes in the lives of nations tempts one almost irresistibly to paradox. Whenever there has been violent revolution, it has always happened that, after the waters of the tempest have subsided, the new society, if it is to survive at all, has to resume many of the features of the old which had been overthrown. There was much of the *ancien régime* restored in the Empire of Napoleon. It is a platitude to-day that Bolshevism is in many matters walking in the footsteps of Peter the Great rather than of Karl Marx. On the other hand, in countries that have not suffered revolution, the meaning of offices, the subtleties of the balance of power have greatly changed over the generations. The critic is tempted to the paradox that all nations are in a continual state of Heraclitan flux save only those that escape it by having a revolution. The only way to keep things the same is to have a revolution about them.

However it may be with the paradox at large, it is certain that Great Britain is the eminent example of the country where the whole balance has changed again and again and is changing to-day without any breach in the formal continuity. "The Republic of Venice alone can compare with it in antiquity", wrote Macaulay of the Papacy a century ago, and, as he noted, the Republic of Venice even then was dead. To-day, unless we count the Papacy as a state, the British is incomparably the oldest state in the world.

It alone of all the States of the modern world traces back its continuity and quotes its precedents from distant centuries, when the whole form of life was different from what it is to-day. The British are accustomed to claim that this continuity is a great strength to them, and so it is. A nation wantonly weakens itself when it shuts itself off from its past. But at the same time he would be making an egregious error, who imagined that because we in England have the same titles which we have had for a 1,000 years that those titles have therefore the same meanings. It is typical of the English, that, though the religious changes which they introduced at the time of the Reformation and in the succeeding century were as radical as those of any Protestant country, yet they were careful to make those changes with the least alteration of ecclesiastical titles. There were bishops after the Reformation as there had been bishops before. There were priests. There were deacons. The words survived. The functions which they denoted largely changed.

I once attended a banquet in celebration of the centenary of the penny postage. Distinguished statesmen were present. Eloquent speeches were made. We were told that the penny postage was a mark of progress. We were bidden to pity our benighted great-great-grandparents who lacked its benefits. It was no wonder we were told, that foreigners who posted in francs or cents or lire did but as they did. Freedom in England broadened down from precedent to precedent. There was indeed only one curious fact of which no mention was made in any of the speeches—the fact that letters now cost 2½d. to post.

This attractive foible is found even in graver matters.

In State, as in Church, we still have kings, as we have had kings for a 1,000 years and more, but he would make very little of English politics who tried to understand them through an assumption that His present Majesty played in the body politic a part in any way analogous to that played by Alfred or by William the Conqueror. Similarly we have had Parliaments for only a few centuries less than we have had kings, but again we should understand very little of England if we imagined that the Parliament of to-day and the Parliament of Simon de Montfort were bodies of a similar constitution and function.

If Parliament traces itself back to these mediaeval origins, Parliamentary government is of course an institution of much more recent growth. In the mediaeval system the king was the real and not merely the nominal head of the executive. He had sufficient income to "live of his own" in normal times. It was only for abnormal adventures that he required to impose taxation and might have to summon Parliament in order to get the money. Parliament had only the very indirect control over general policy which the negative power to withhold abnormal supplies gave to it. Even such a control it was often unable to exercise, and most notably so in Tudor times, when Kings in England, like other Renaissance princes, were able greatly to increase the monarchical power.

Then in the seventeenth century a rise in prices, owing to the influx of American gold, far steeper than the rise in rents, caused the King's expenditure to increase much more rapidly than his income. He was no longer able to live of his own and in independence of taxation. This, and the religious difference and other issues, brought on the Civil War, in which Parliament gained the victory over the King. The Parliamentary victory opened the way for Parliamentary government. It opened the way for it. It did not at once introduce it, either formally or informally. Cromwell was in no sense a Parliamentary Prime Minister nor was his Government in any sense a Parliamentary Government. After Cromwell's death Charles II returned to the throne. His reign was a reign of unstable equilibrium, Charles neither accepted nor outspokenly rejected the Parliamentary claims to sovereignty. He preferred to work against them indirectly, but, so long as the Stuarts were on the throne, it certainly could not be said that the issue was settled or that England was under Parliamentary government in any modern sense of the phrase.

After 1688 the issue was perhaps at last settled. Yet even after 1688 not only William III but even Anne continued to exercise many royal prerogatives, which it would not be thinkable that a modern sovereign should exercise. These sovereigns, for instance, continued to preside at their own Cabinet meetings and we are often told that the modern constitution took its form when Walpole established himself as the first Prime Minister two hundred years before the title received any formal recognition, by presiding at Cabinet meetings in place of George I, who knew no English. The example is a valid one. The anecdote, so often told to suggest that things `happen in England by irrelevant accident, in reality proves exactly the opposite. There was nothing odd in the world of the eighteenth century in a monarch being ignorant of the language of the country of which he was the ruler. In another country all that would have happened would have been that the ministers would have had to learn their monarch's language. The fact that they did not do so in England was not the cause of the monarch's decline but the proof that the Ministers were already more important than the monarch— that the Government was already a Parliamentary rather than a monarchical government.

But Parliamentary government is not of course necessarily democratic government. It is of the essence of a Parliament that it is a representative body, but whom it represents at any given moment is as it may be. It can only be called a democratic body if it is elected by something approximating to universal suffrage, and on that test the governments of the eighteenth century were clearly anything but democratic. They would have been profoundly shocked if anybody had called them democratic. The revolution of 1688 established what Lord Acton called "the divine right of freeholders" and power throughout the eighteenth century was held firmly in the hands of the Whig aristocracy. Even after the Reform Bill of 1832 the country was in no sense democratic. All that that reform did was to transfer power from the old aristocracy to the new capitalist middle class. It was only after the second Reform Bill of 1867 that the country had for the first time a constitution that could in any way be called democratic. The town-worker then received the vote, though not yet the agricultural worker. The agriculturalist did not receive the vote until the Third Reform Bill of 1884. Thenceforward it was possible to say that the country enjoyed something approaching universal suffrage, subject only to one large reservation—that votes were still confined to males. If the family is the unit and democracy only demands one family one vote, then we may say that Britain was a democracy from 1884. If the requisite principle is one adult one vote, then the country only became a democracy with the enfranchisement of women in 1918.

All this is a familiar story. What is not quite so widely understood is that there has been a change over the centuries in the nature of parties not dissimilar to the change over the centuries in the nature of Parliament. As long as there was real monarchical government, there were no parties in Parliament in anything like the modern sense. Parliament as a whole was ranged against the King in defence of its own interests. It is true that, when the clash came between King and Parliament in Charles I's reign, grave divisions were found in Parliament, as they were in the nation at large. The Grand Remonstrance, for instance, was only passed by eleven votes.[1] Nevertheless the sides did not form themselves into regular parties in the modern sense. Parties made their appearance as a consequence—and probably an inevitable consequence—of the passage of effective sovereignty to Parliament. As long as it was still at issue whether Parliament should be sovereign, then, whatever their incidental differences, all members of Parliament were substantially united in supporting its claim. But, as soon as it was conceded that Parliament should have power, then at once members quarrelled with one another how they should use that power.

[1] It was passed by 159 votes to 148. What is interesting is the smallness of the division—307 members out of a total of 558.

Regular Parliamentary parties first made their appearance in English history in the reign of Charles II. The two parties were the Whigs and the Tories—each so christened in nickname by their opponents. A Whig was originally a Scottish highwayman and a Tory was an Irish pirate who inhabited the Tory Islands some miles off the coast of Co. Donegal.[1] The first issue that divided the parties was that of the Exclusion Bill, designed to exclude James, Duke of York, from the succession to the throne on the death of Charles II on account of his profession of the Catholic religion; yet, even then, though there were parties, there was no party government in quite the modern sense. The King, since he also was opposed to his brother's exclusion from the throne, naturally sympathized with the Tories against the Whigs, and Shaftesbury, the great Whig leader, was his primal enemy. Yet Charles had his own game to play and the party strife within Parliament was still but one aspect of the large attempt of the monarchy to regain for itself at any rate a portion of its real power.

Charles was for the moment successful and the Exclusion Bill was defeated. James was able to ascend the throne, but he soon succeeded in alienating politicians of all parties and the invitation to William III to supplant him was signed by both Whigs and Tories. It was William's intention to rule through a Ministry in which Whigs and Tories were balanced against one another, but the accident that the Whigs supported his Dutch ambition of war on France and the Tories opposed it in time forced him into the arms of the Whigs.

The conflict between Whigs and Tories, which had first been joined on the question whether James II should be allowed to succeed Charles II, found its second clear issue a generation later on the question whether James's son, the

---

[1] It is a curiosity that the original Irish Tories were Catholics who refused to allow Cromwell to expel them to Connaught. The Orangemen were, as their name of course implies, Whigs. It is one of the strangest oddities of history that the modern Ulster Unionist should sometimes be called a Tory.

Old Pretender, should be allowed to succeed his daughter Anne, or whether the succession should rather go to the nearest Protestant heir, their distant cousin, George, the Elector of Hanover. The establishment of George upon the throne marked, as we have argued, the definite establishment of Parliamentary government, for George was the first of our sovereigns who did not exercise even that minimum of influence which was necessary if one was to say that the Crown was still a challenger to the theory of Parliamentary sovereignty. But, if the succession of George marked the establishment of Parliamentary government, it did not at all mark the establishment of party government. To the contrary. The Tory leader, Bolingbroke, had in Queen Anne's day put forward his theory of "a Patriot King", in which he had pleaded for a balance in the state between an independent monarch and an independent Parliament. The King, he argued, should on no account be the mere nominee or servant of Parliament. He must hold his office in his own right. It is his duty to check the Parliament when, as sometimes happens, the Parliament misrepresents the interests of the nation and the wishes of its constituents. On such a theory it was clearly improper for Parliament to attempt to regulate the succession to the throne at all. Prince James should have succeeded automatically and without question in virtue of his possession of the better hereditary claim.

It followed obviously from that that, once the Hanoverian succession was established, the Tories were necessarily suspect. Every Tory was bound either to be an overt Jacobite or at the least to have accepted the Hanoverian succession only in a reluctant spirit and as one accepts an ugly fact. So long as the Hanoverian dynasty persisted, Tories could not expect office. The result was that Tory leaders in those years indulged, as bold Conservatives out of office often do, in surprisingly radical demands. Shippen, the Tory leader of the days of Walpole's régime, one of the interesting forgotten men of English history, was the first English politician to demand a radical reform of the

Parliamentary franchise and distribution of seats—and this demand was put forward by the Tories and opposed by the Whigs a century before it was put forward by the Whigs and opposed by the Tories in 1832.

But the battle for office in the reigns of the first two Georges was fought out not between Whigs and Tories, but between Whigs and Whigs. All the office-holders of those two reigns were, and quite inevitably must have been, Whigs. In the battles by which ministers were put up and pulled down, personality and principle played their mingled parts. But the leaders had not a party of their own to which to appeal. They had rather to seek to win a majority within a party that was in any event dominant. It is true that within the Whig party there did spring up various groups, such as "the Boys", as the group that acted with Pitt in his attack on Walpole was called. But these groups, though they had about them some of the passing marks of party, could not truly be called political parties. Their organization was not sufficiently definite to earn them such a title, and above all they did not aspire to that continuity of life to which a political party always aspires, hoping as it does to outlive the issues of the moment. The Boys acted together in order to unseat Walpole and never pretended that they would continue to act together once Walpole was unseated.

With the accession of George III in 1760 we find something that could more plausibly claim to be called party government. After the defeat of the Jacobite rebellion of 1745 there was no longer any serious question of the overthrow of the Hanoverian dynasty, and those who wished for a strengthening of the monarchical power were now content to see it strengthened in the hands of the present occupant of the throne, and did not demand that the chances of a real success be sacrificed to the demands of an abstract logic by raising once more the question of the succession. George III was willing that the attempt should be made under his leadership.

George's first attempt was made through the agency of his tutor, Lord Bute. This was a purely personal attempt and Bute could hardly be said to be the leader of a political party, but George learnt his lesson from Bute's failure. The lesson that he learnt was that Parliament was now so power-ful that it could only be undermined from within. In order to re-establish the monarch's personal power it was necessary for him to build up a party within Parliament which would support him in his endeavour. Therefore George created within Parliament the party of the "King's Friends", who were willing to support the King in the same way as the clients of the Great Whig noblemen were willing to support their patrons. The King's Friends were recruited partly from those who by patriotic conviction thought it to be to the national advantage that the monarchical interest should be strengthened and partly—as was the way in the eighteenth century—by placemen and nominees from rotten boroughs, who supported the King just as others supported their Whig patrons, because it was to the interest of their pockets to do so.

It was this party of the King's Friends which supported and kept in office the Government of Lord North between 1770 and 1782, and it may be said that here were the beginnings of party government—between a regular Govern-ment party acting in support of the Government in accord-ance with a disciplined programme and the regular Parliamentary opposition of the Whigs. But it was, of course, party government of a different type from the party government of the next century—in at any rate one very important particular. Whereas it was the essence of Victorian party government that both parties loyally accepted the Parliamentary system and contended with one another only to settle who should be the Government within that system, the King's Friends were, of course, challenging the system and trying to undermine it from within.

The test of Lord North's Government was the American War. Had North's Government conducted that war with exemplary efficiency, had it been able to point a contrast between its patriotic vigour and the dilatory incompetence of its Whig predecessors, then it is possible that the British people might have been persuaded that its interests were more truly served by a monarchical than by an aristocratic Parliamentary Government. But, when its efforts ended in dismal failure, then it was evident that whatever the faults of corruption and incompetence of the Whigs, this remedy to them was worse than the disease. After the surrender at Yorktown Lord North fell from power.

Yet George was not wholly defeated in his efforts to assert himself. In the next years he was able successfully to defy and to dismiss the coalition of Fox and North and to establish in their place his own nominee, the younger Pitt. His choice was ratified by the electorate and Pitt was able to hold power for eighteen years. Yet Pitt's Government was in no sense the personal government of the King. The King in no way dictated its policy. Indeed for a portion of its rule, as for the greater part of the rest of his life, George III was insane.[1] Nor were the lines of division during Pitt's régime in any way regular party lines. Fox, his main opponent, was the leader of the Whigs, but Pitt also called himself a Whig up till the day of his death. North, with whom Fox had been in coalition immediately before Pitt came to power, was the leader of the Tories. Burke, the secretary of Rockingham, considered himself at the beginning of Pitt's rule to be of the strictest sect of Whigs, but at the coming of the French Revolution he and the other Portland Whigs deserted Fox and moved over to the support of Pitt in the French War. So during Pitt's time party loyalties were in inextricable confusion and statesmen had to justify their policies to the individual member on their intrinsic merits. The overwhelming majority of Parliament supported Pitt in his French war, but they did not form any definite party to support him.

Yet in the years after Pitt's death the parties of the nineteenth century formed themselves round this issue of the French war. Those who supported the war formed the

---

[1] When it comes to that, in 1802 every hereditary monarch in Europe was, Bagehot reminds us, insane.

Tory party of the nineteenth century—which was in many ways quite a different party from the Tory party of the eighteenth century—and those who opposed it formed the Whig party. The restoration of independent monarchical power was no longer in question, and except for two or three minor interventions—William IV's dismissal of Melbourne in 1834, Queen Victoria's refusal to allow Peel to make changes among her women of the Bedchamber in 1839—the Sovereign never more attempted a direct interference with the course of policy. Both parties accepted the Parliamentary system. The nineteenth century saw the full establishment both of Parliamentary and of party government.

CHAPTER III

THE NEW STATE

YET, EVEN SO, party government in the first half of the
nineteenth century meant something very different
from party government to-day. Though Britain had
Parliamentary government in those days, yet, as has
already been noted, she by no means had democratic
government, and from the plutocratic nature of government
and from the predominant *laissez-faire* philosophy certain
consequences flowed which made Parliament and party
alike to be words of very different meaning from those which
they bear to-day. There was, of course, in those days no
payment of members. There was even during the earlier
half of the century a property qualification for members
of Parliament. With but a few exceptions, the members
of Parliament were persons of independent means, and there
was no general feeling among the governing class that it was
in the public interest to smooth the way for those who were
not of independent means to become members. On the
other hand the vast majority of human activities were
deliberately left outside the control and interference of the
State. The State was thought of as the organ of private
interest that would inevitably act, should it be allowed to
act at all, in a private interest. It is, of course, an error to
think of the age of *laissez-faire* as an age of no rules. It was
an age of very strict rules but they were rules imposed by
the members of a profession on one another. Take, for
instance, the City of London and the Stock Exchange—
the very Mecca of *laissez-faire*. Their members accepted the
most exact and elaborate code of professional etiquette,
imposed by themselves upon themselves, and unchallenged
and severe punishment followed any violation of that code.
So, too, in the world of medicine or in the world of law.
In industry and in commerce, too, there was a professional

ette, if not quite so exactly defined—methods of business competition which were regarded as unethical, though some of them, may be, were not explicitly forbidden by any Act of Parliament. The punishment for violation of the code was not, save in exceptional circumstances, prosecution by the Courts. It was the refusal by other people to "do business with a chap who does things like that". That was thought to be the better plan. The public interest was best served on the Benthamite philosophy by preventing state interference. The road of progress was the road of an ever diminishing state interference. The Factory Acts, and other such acts, as won their way on to the Statute Book, won their way there explicitly as exceptions, as remedies against the very grossest abuses and usually even then in face of the strongest opposition.

The members of Parliament are to-day drawn from a much wider circle than were the members of a hundred years ago, and it might appear from a simple mathematical calculation, combined with an equally simple interpretation of the doctrine of the equality of man, that if members of Parliament are drawn impartially from the whole population they should be forty times as able as they were when they were drawn from only one fortieth of the population. But it would in truth be very difficult to maintain that the level of ability in Parliament has risen at all with the extension of the franchise and quite impossible to maintain that it has risen in any way in proportion to the increase in the electorate's number.

Why not? It would not be difficult to suggest a number of reasons, but certainly the question cannot be intelligently answered unless we first understand in what way the Parliament of the last century was a different body from the Parliament of to-day. Members were not dependent on their Parliamentary membership for their income; in fact, it was always greatly to their financial advantage to lose their seats. What was perhaps even more important—the greater number were not dependent on their Parliamentary membership for their prestige in society. To-day there are very few members of Parliament so distinguished outside its walls that their prestige is not a little enhanced by their possession of a seat and would not be a little diminished by their loss of it. In the England of a hundred years ago, with the immense prestige of the landed gentry, things were different. It mattered little to a landowner of a county family of the first rank whether he was also incidentally a member of Parliament. He was what he was, and he held his position in society in virtue of what he was. His reputation was above the accidents of success and failure, of capture or achievement.

It is no part of my thesis at this moment to defend such an arrangement of society and certainly no part of my thesis to deny that, like all arrangements, it had its faults and injustices and, like all things human, carried within itself the seeds of its own destruction. Yet it had its consequences, consequences which it is important to note, whether for approval or disapproval. Personally I happen somewhat to dislike aristocratic societies, but the complaint against the modern democrat is not that he rejects the case for aristocracy but that he does not know what it is.

The consequence of an aristocratic hierarchy was that the ordinary member of Parliament claimed and obtained a degree of personal freedom which would be quite inconceivable to his modern descendant. The Parliamentary debate was, it is true, as a rule, carried on by the half a dozen chosen gladiators of each side. There was none of the modern press of all sorts and conditions of members to "get in" at a debate. I should imagine—I do not know if there is any exact statistic available—that there must have been a very high proportion of the members of Parliament in the eighteenth century or the first three quarters of the last century, who, like Gibbon and Addison, never delivered even a maiden speech. Nor was it either humility or timidity which was responsible for their silence. It was much more likely to be pride. They would not demean themselves by offering their observations to an assembly, and, as for the modern notion that their constituents would like to read their speeches, they would have stood astounded at such impertinence. "As for living", said de l'Isle Adam, "our servants will do that for us", and as for speechifying and the day-to-day government of the country and other such activities, the country gentleman of the early nineteenth century was quite willing to leave such plebeian exercises to *parvenus arrivistes* such as a Peel, a Gladstone or a Disraeli. Like Trollope's Sir Walter Waxless, "he had never opened his mouth" in Parliament. . . . "But he was Sir Walter Waxless, and what with his tailor and what with his eyebrows he did command a great deal of respect." When a real gentleman such as Melbourne or Palmerston took his hand at governing the country, he did so in a somewhat consciously comic fashion as if he knew that he was slightly lowering himself, as when he danced at the servants' ball. If he was in opposition, then, like Grey, he went off to his country estate, and it was only what was to him the intolerable insult of the repeal of the Corn Laws, which roused one of the greatest orators of that century, Lord George Bentinck, to speak at all in the House of Commons, in which he had previously sat for years but in whose debates it had never occurred to him that a gentleman should intervene. Speaking in Parliament was to him an occupation like taking one's children to the sea-side—an occupation which marked one as of the middle-class.

All this it may be said was somewhat absurd—and so indeed taken in isolation it is, as are all social habits when taken out in isolation from the general surrounding in which they are set. Pride in all its forms is always ridiculous, but at least it can be tolerated, when it is not fanatical. The case for an aristocratic Parliament is this—and it is not a bad case. There must always be a degree of insincerity in the profession of an egalitarian creed by a politician, because the member of Parliament receives, and very rapidly comes to expect, a slightly enhanced consideration because of his position. He rarely goes to a meeting without being on the platform. He is usually a speaker. His name is constantly in the papers, and so on. He is talked about and noticed, and, if he is honest, he admits that he likes being talked about and noticed. And this consideration is a much more dangerous form of inequality than the accident of possessing a little more money than your neighbour. Members of Parliament are always open to the charge, "If you really believe in equality why are you a member of Parliament at all?" And only those of the deepest sincerity or the deepest insincerity can meet such a charge with total confidence. For that reason there is something to be said for drawing members of Parliament from a class whose head is not easily turned by consideration because it receives consideration of its own right anyway, just as, admittedly, there is much to be said on the other side.

The mystical and theological doctrine of the equality of man is a profound truth, and this truth has indeed its consequences in the secular sphere. It makes injustice to be intolerable. But the fact that all men are equal in the sight of God does not make them equal in the sight of man. However much an easy cant may sometimes find it convenient to pretend a belief in that doctrine, no one in fact believes it. The vast majority of men are sensibly content to accept the position in life into which they find themselves born and rightly feel that they would merely condemn themselves to unhappiness were they to tie themselves down to a life of envy and unceasing competition. A few on the other hand feel—and rightly feel—that they have special gifts and vocation to serve mankind in a larger sphere than that into which they were born. Their ambition is laudable, but it is certainly not equalitarian. I remember well a friend of mine, a Socialist leader, telling me how he could not repress a feeling of envy and bitterness in the company of those who had had better educational chances than he—how he felt it his duty to better himself in order that he might help those who lacked his abilities. It was all intelligible and honourable and modestly sincere, and when we consider the insolence of a certain type of wearer of the Old School Tie, his bland assumption that preference for all desirable jobs must necessarily be given to people who were at school with him, one cannot but sympathize with the resentment of those who were born outside the charmed circle. Yet my Socialist friend did not for a moment believe that men were equal. He merely believes that the inequalities had been wrongly arranged.

One result of an aristocratic Parliament was that there was a far greater freedom in the division lobbies than would be imagined possible to-day. In the first place Parliament only sat for a small part of the year—the essential condition according to Burke's wise judgement if Parliamentary government was to be tolerable. The greater part of their lives members spent in the company of those who were not politicians. Members of Parliament were under no temptation to form a professional union, bound together with ties that transcend their nominal differences of opinion, to defend a system that is greatly to their advantage against an uncomprehending world of constituents that sneer at it— which is the great danger of the modern professional politician. "There is more in common", said a witty French cynic, "between two deputies one of whom is a Communist than there is between two Communists one of whom is a deputy."

The Bills that were introduced were few. For those who cared so to occupy their leisure there was ample of it to master what was in those Bills. The matter of them— Catholic Emancipation, a Reform Bill, even the Repeal of the Corn Laws—was matter upon which any educated man could form an opinion of his own, for what it might be worth. The Government did not find it necessary to monopolize even the limited time during which Parliament sat—from February usually until June. Private members had their time and their opportunity to introduce measures of their own. For instance, as Mr. G. M. Young tells us in his *Essay on a Victorian Centenary*, in the last session of King William IV's reign Parliament met on eighty-eight days out of the three-hundred and sixty five. On one day it went home for lack of a quorum. On seven days it was counted out. There were twenty-eight days of Government business.

The rest was private members' time. Nor was it found necessary to curtail debate. The closure was unknown. There was no such thing as taking the committee stage of a Bill "upstairs" in a Standing Committee. Every clause of every Bill could be fully debated on the floor of the House and every member who wished to do so could speak on it.

In such an atmosphere there were, of course, political parties and party government, but it is very important not to be misled by a mere verbalism into thinking that the party system in that day meant at all the same thing as it means to-day. Since the Tory party of the nineteenth century derived its ancestry from the younger Pitt, who had lived and died calling himself a Whig, it was not surprising that the politicians of that day felt little of an obligation to choose one side and to stick to it through life. Derby, Palmerston, Gladstone—all were found at one time on the one side and at another on the other side of the House. Gladstone's passage from Toryism to Liberalism was, it is true, gradual and principled and followed logically, if not inevitably, from his support of Peel in the Repeal of the Corn Laws but it would be hard to find any deeper principle which led Palmerston to be a Tory in his youth and a Whig or Liberal in his old age than the accident that the Tories were in power in his youth and the Whigs were in power in his old age. Lord Melbourne, though a chance of heredity caused him to be a Member of the Whig Government which passed the first Reform Bill, yet never made any pretence of believing in that Bill.

An independent member, said the Lord Derby of that day, is a member who cannot be depended on. Why this truism should have been considered to be a joke, I have never been able to understand, and there were in the Parliaments of those days a much larger number of independent members than we find in a modern Parliament. They did not, it is true, call themselves independent members. The imposed Parliamentary discipline was so lax that it was not necessary to do so, but a country gentleman, who owed his election to his family name in his locality, had no need to obey a

party whip, nor was party fanaticism likely to cause him
to do so, as the differences between the parties were not such
that anyone could seriously think that the country would
be ruined by the accession of one party to power or necessarily
saved by the accession of the other. The pattern of elections
was very different from that of to-day. Members of the same
party stood against one another, indifferent that they might
thus present the seat to a third candidate of the other party.
In the election of 1874 twenty-five Conservatives owed their
victory to the fact that two Liberals stood against each
of them in their constituencies and thus let them in on split
votes. Or, if we go back thirty-seven years behind that, we
find that, at the General Election of 1837, out of the six
hundred odd seats in only two hundred and ten of them were
there contests and of those two hundred and ten, sixty-seven
were challenged by petitions.

Trollope was an accurate observer. His creation,
Plantagenet Palliser, was a politician ambitious for office.
Yet he was in Parliament for some time before he even
chose his party. As Trollope puts it, "The world said that
he was a rising man and old Nestor of the Cabinet looked
on him as one who would be able at some far future day
to come among them as a younger brother. Hitherto he
had declined such inferior offices as had been offered to
him, biding his time carefully; and he was as yet tied hand
and neck to no party, though known to be Liberal in his
political tendencies."

Therefore the party leader had little hold save over the
small number of members who were deeply ambitious of
office. We tend to read history through the biographies
of history's leading figures and therefore we exaggerate the
prevalence of ambition. But the truth is that, though many
men are willing to take office if it comes to them and though
a defiant, persisting *nolo episcopari* is perhaps not very
common, yet that little kink of unbalance which drives a
man to the sacrifice of all the amenities of life to the proble-
matical satisfaction of ambitions of political office is equally
uncommon. Many people would like to be Prime Minister,

but only quite a few people are willing to take the trouble required to become Prime Minister.

The world has been saved again and again by the laziness of its politicians. We tend to forget those unremembered names which we find in country churchyards, of whom are recorded a number of unhonourable and undistinguished achievements and among them "M.P. for Barsetshire 1832-1837". Yet throughout all its history Parliament has been kept alive by its back-benchers, and in the early nineteenth century the undistinguished and unambitious members for Barsetshire greatly outnumbered the Peels and Disraelis and Palmerstons. No party contributed to their election expenses and as a result no party could control their votes in the division lobby. In the eighteenth century they had been controlled by their noble patrons. Perhaps even in the nineteenth century the great landowners had undue power in the country but they had less than they had had previously, whereas the new masters of our own day had not yet risen to their tyranny. As a result Parliament between the first and the second Reform Bills—between 1832 and 1867—was probably freer in its voting and debating than it has ever been before or since. On none of the great issues of the day could the Government be sure before the division how the voting would go or even whether they would carry the day. The Reform Bill, the Corn Laws, the Conspiracy to Murder Bill, the "tit for tat" with John Russell—these debates mark a level of Parliamentary freedom, unparalleled in previous history and from which all subsequent history has been a decline. The ordinary member did not speak in debate. He left speaking to the leaders, but he came and listened and gave his vote—to an extent quite incomprehensible to-day—on the merits of the debate. The debate was the thing. The debate mattered. Government really was Parliamentary government—much more truly than it is to-day.

It can of course most fairly be argued that Parliament was only able to preserve this freedom from business and consequent independence by the fact that the State refrained from doing many things that it ought to have done. It is the condition of Parliamentary government that there should be no strong government, and under the rule of *laissez-faire* many evils grew rank which the strong arm of Government should have controlled. Without embarking on the controversy what degree of industrial control was ideally required by the conditions of the nineteenth century, yet I am far from disputing the legitimacy of this argument. It is not my thesis that no sacrifice is too great for the preservation of Parliamentary freedom. It is my thesis only that that freedom easily survives in a society in which certain policies are pursued and that its survival under other policies is a great deal more difficult.

It is well said in Monypenny and Buckle that the great age of Parliament substantially corresponded with Disraeli's membership of it. I think that that is true, and, if true, it must be added that Disraeli's was also the hand which dealt the first blow to that Parliamentary freedom. The nature of the electorate was substantially changed by the Reform Bill of 1867. The town-working man was given the vote. It had been Disraeli's confident hope that the working-man would show his gratitude to the Conservatives who had given him the franchise by voting Conservative in the election of that year. He did not do so. The electorate returned a Liberal majority. The lesson which Disraeli imagined himself to have learnt from that reverse was that there was now a new sort of electorate which must be wooed with new tactics. The old, careless, easy-going ways were no longer sufficient. There must be a definite, nation-wide party organization under a central office—an institution till then unknown in our political life. Disraeli's tactics were immediately successful and in the election of 1874 the Conservatives won a notable victory. But it was hardly to be expected that such success would not find imitators. If the Conservatives had organized, why should not the Liberals organize, too? Joseph Chamberlain had already organized Birmingham in the Radical interest. He now adopted all the lessons which he could learn from American practice and extended the principles of his Birmingham organization to the Liberals of all the country. The result was that the pendulum swung back and in 1880 the elections went to the Liberals. Within the Liberal party the Radical wing, to whom such tactics were more easily native, gained at the expense of the old Whigs, and indeed the Liberal partly would probably have become a purely Radical party before the end of the 1880's, had not the whole alignment been changed by the secession from it of Joseph Chamberlain on Home Rule in the middle of that decade.

That introduction by Disraeli into the Conservative party and by Chamberlain into the Liberal party of a regular party machinery greatly changed the nature of political parties. Each party still had, it is true, eccentric, semi-independent members who relied for their election upon local popularity and who cared nothing for headquarters and party organization. But for the first time it became a substantial advantage to be recognized as an official candidate, and this gave a power to Whips and party organizers which they had never before possessed. It was now for the first time possible to frighten a member with an effective threat that, if his conduct was too undisciplined, the whip would be withdrawn from him.

Disraeli and Chamberlain had a third and yet stranger companion who shared with them the responsibility in these years for the restriction of Parliamentary freedom. A free system of Parliament can only survive so long as all members are genuinely anxious that the system should work. It is possible to allow to every member the right to speak to every motion so long as that right is only exercised by those who have truly something to say. If every member attempted to exercise this right on every motion, Parliamentary life would soon become impossible. Now throughout the first three-quarters of the nineteenth century it was broadly true that Parliament consisted only of members who had a sincere interest in seeing the system work. There were, of course, a few, individual, eccentric exceptions—such, for instance, as Dr. Kenealy, who got himself elected as the member for Stoke-on-Trent as a supporter of the Tichborne Claimant, introduced himself into the House and hung his umbrella on the mace while he was taking the oath; or the atheist, Bradlaugh, who filled these latter years with the controversy whether he had the right to affirm instead of taking the oath. But broadly it was true that all members of Parliament of those days were either supporters of the Government of the day or else supporters of a party which had a reasonable hope of one day becoming the Government. This was true even of the Radicals who, though they disassociated themselves from the mid-Victorian Whigs, had yet no ambition save that of one distant day attaining power with a Parliamentary majority.

But from the first the Irish members were different from the members of any of the regular British parties. The Union of 1800 had only been passed through the Irish Parliament by the use of much bribery and blackmail. That Irish Parliament had no sort of mandate from its electors to vote itself out of existence. In so far as the Union was in any sort of sense accepted by any responsible section of the Irish people, it was accepted as a part of a bargain the other condition of which was Catholic Emancipation. That bargain owing to George III's objections was not kept and the Catholics had to wait another twenty-nine years for their emancipation.

In any event, whatever the strength of these arguments, the point for the moment relevant is that the Irish Nationalists did not recognize the moral validity of the Union and wished to end it as soon as possible. This put the Irish Nationalist member at Westminster into an entirely different position from that of a member of any other party. The members of other parties, whether they supported the Government of the moment or not, at least wished the system to continue and to work well, hoping for a day when they would have a Government to their liking. But the Irish Nationalists had, of course, no motive to wish well to the system. Rather was it to their interest to demonstrate that the system could not possibly work until the Irish

members were given their freedom to depart from Westminster and to legislate for themselves in Dublin.

In the 1870's the Irish Nationalist party was under the
leadership of Isaac Butt, a mild-mannered lawyer, who did
not push his case to its full logical extremities. He contented
himself with introducing year by year academic resolutions
in favour of Irish Home Rule into the House of Commons
—resolutions which were, of course, overwhelmingly defeated.
But in the 1880's Butt was succeeded in the leadership by
Parnell—a man of a very different temperament. Parnell
saw that the life of the House of Commons was from one
point of view a game and that, like all games, it could easily
be made ridiculous if players took strict advantage of the
letter of every privilege allowed to them by the rules.
Every member had the right to speak on every motion.
Once a member was in the possession of the floor of the
House, there was no power in the Speaker or anybody
else to compel him to sit down until he wished to do
so.

Therefore it was not difficult for the Irish members to
make certain that, if the grievances of Ireland were not
attended to, at least nobody else's grievances would be
attended to either. All that they had to do was, one after
another, to make enormous speeches on every topic that
came up, whether it genuinely engaged their interest or not,
and the whole legislative machinery was held up. Parliament had to defend itself with a reply to such tactics, and
therefore rules of debate were introduced which created a
machinery by which debates could be cut short by closure.
Such rules, as a defence of the House against deliberate
obstruction, were clearly only in a formal sense violations
of Parliamentary freedom; in reality they were rules in
support of Parliamentary freedom, but the proof that the
times were changing was that these rules, once adopted,
were not adopted as provisional emergency regulations.
When Gladstone took up the cause of Home Rule, the Irish
party ceased to obstruct as a permanent and deliberate
policy. No party has ever obstructed as a permanent and

deliberate policy since then—yet the rules of closure remain.

What is the reason for this? It may be maintained that the spirit of liberty has declined, that liberty is an aristocratic taste, that democratic institutions only work in aristocratic societies, that the discipline of party has grown more strict, that with payment of members and with the member who looks upon politics as his career the party machine has in this century a far greater hold over the member than it had in the last century. All these contentions are most defensible and may well all be true. Spengler advanced it as a general law that, as the electorate is enlarged, the power of Parliament must inevitably decline. Whether it be a general law or not, it is certainly what has happened in England. But clearly, whatever may be said about the particular restrictions on Parliamentary debate, the basic question is—should Parliament do so much? The nineteenth-century Parliament was able to preserve its freedom of debate because it only attempted to control a very small portion of the national life. The twentieth-century Parliament attempts to control a vastly greater portion of that life—indeed considers that the whole of that life is a proper subject for its supervision, and, if Parliament is going to take upon itself so boundless a function, it can only perform it—if "perform" be the right word —if its traditional privileges are very closely circumscribed. If we are going to have the volume of legislation that modern taste demands, then we must have, if not precisely the same restrictions on our freedom as at present, at the least a great many restrictions. Bagehot wrote as long ago as 1868, "The great defect of the House of Commons is that it has no leisure. The life of the House is the worst of all lives— a life of distracting routine." If that is what he thought eighty years ago, what would he have thought to-day? The question really is then—do we want so many laws?

Before we close with the problem of to-day, let us first be careful to get it into its right proportion. Both supporters and opponents of the present Socialist Government tend to be united in a conspiracy to pretend that the problem is a great deal newer than it really is. It is new only in its degree. The rules of closure dated back to the 1880's and were never repealed. The Liberal Government of 1906-1914 embarked upon a programme which, if it left the area of legislation much smaller than it is to-day, nevertheless greatly extended it beyond any area that had been covered by any of its predecessors. The war of 1914 brought, of course, a vast further extension of legislation, as did the last war, but it was not necessary to restrict the freedom of Parliament in order to enact that legislation. The war had brought a suspension of party warfare and during the second half of the war Coalition Governments were in power. Legislation does not require the artificial assistance of a closure to enable it to move quickly when it is unopposed, or even, as a rule, when the opposition is of a few individuals and not of an organized party.

We often hear people speaking of the years between the wars as years of uninterrupted *laissez-faire*. Such terms are relative. Though the Governments of those days may have appeared to do little by the standards of the Government of to-day, they would certainly have appeared to do criminally much by the standards of our ancestors. As a matter of fact, if we apply a crudely statistical test, the Parliament of 1918 in the first two years of its life passed more Acts than the Parliament of 1945 in its first two years. Admittedly those Acts were not in general of as far-reaching importance and they passed through Parliament with ease and without the need of exceptional restriction on debate because of the weakness or absence of opposition. The election of 1918 had returned a Parliament almost unanimously pledged to the support of the Lloyd George Coalition Government. The opposition was divided between the Labour party, the Asquithian Liberals and five relics of the old Redmondite Irish Nationalist parties. Of these the Liberals and the Irish were vigorous in opposition but their numbers were not sufficient to make them effective. The Labour party was more numerous and had established itself for the first time

as the official opposition, but it was not yet capable of its
new responsibilities.   Its opposition was feebly and in-
effectively conducted.   The weakness of opposition during
those all-important years certainly left its strong mark on the
face of legislation.   It was twenty years before a Socialist
Government had come into power that Lord Hewart wrote
his book, *The New Despotism*, denouncing the decline of
liberty and in particular the growing habit of legislation by
delegation, by which Parliament, instead of making the
law directly, delegated to somebody else the right to issue
a regulation.

The those who like cynically to meditate how wheels turn
full circles and politicians change their views with their
opportunity could hardly divert themselves better than by
going to the British Museum and there obtaining a copy
of a rare little book called *The Great Food Riots*, 1890.   This
book is one of those imaginative reconstructions of the future,
in which the Victorians delighted.   Really written in 1885,
it pretends to be written in 1934 and to be dedicated to
the author's grandson.   It describes how "a certain noble
lord, once a member for a pocket borough but later the
champion and representative of Tory democracy in the
Midland metropolis", was going to break with the older
parties and, in alliance with the Trade Unions, found the
National Labour Protection League.   This new Labour party
under the Lord's leadership was, it is pretended, to fight
and win the election of 1889, gaining a majority of seats
though only a minority of votes.   It is to come into office
on a programme of fair trade, or protection, of a gigantic
housing programme and of the control of the rate of interest
at $2\frac{1}{2}$ per cent.   The protectionist policy leads to famine.
The result of the housing programme is that labour is
drained off from the mines and textiles, where production
disastrously declines, and cheap money ends in fiasco.
In the second year of its power—1890—there are shortages
of food and bread riots in Trafalgar Square.   The mob
storms down Whitehall and expels the Government.

The author of this book who chooses this literary device

to pillory all interferences with the absolute principles of *laissez faire* and to prophesy their catastrophe was St. Loe Strachey, the father of the present Minister of Food. The "noble lord", of whom the author prophesied that he would be the founder of the Labour party and the introducer of Socialism, was Lord Randolph Churchill.

CHAPTER IV

POST-SOCIALISM

CONTROVERSIES ABOUT the innovations and restrictions of the present Socialist Government are apt to end in a quarrel which may have its validity within the purely party debate but which is profoundly unsatisfactory to the impartial guardian of traditional liberty. The Conservative levels his accusation against some Socialist restriction, and the Socialist replies by pointing to some action of a pre-war Conservative Government in which he alleges a valid precedent. The controversy rages whether the two cases are parallel. Now, if we really believe that this country was an entirely Conservative and traditional country up till 1939, then that is a thoroughly pertinent controversy, but, if we rather believe—which is manifestly the truth—that society had been undergoing a gradual transformation ever since the first World War and in some ways since an even earlier date and that the Socialist accession to power in 1945 was only the culmination of a process, then it is not particularly important to discover that the Conservatives of the years before the war often set precedents which were copied by the Socialists of the years after the war, for all were going, willy-nilly, in the same direction. But whether it was a right direction is a wholly different question.

To show that this is no exclusively party matter, let us take our example of the evil from a period of Conservative rule. Section 67 of the Rating and Valuation Act, 1925, which Lord Hewart cites, is entitled "Power to Remove Difficulties". It provides that, if any difficulties arise "in bringing into operation any of the provisions of this Act" the Minister "may by order remove the difficulty". He may "constitute any assessment committee, or declare any assessment committee to be duly constituted or make any appointment, or do any other thing which appears to him necessary or expedient for seeing the due preparation of the list or for bringing the said provisions into operation". And, if that is not enough, "any such order may modify the provisions of this Act so far as may appear to the Minister necessary or expedient for carrying the order into effect". This is but one example of hundreds that could be cited, alike from Conservative and from Socialist legislation. It is clear that, so long as provisions of this nature are being placed upon the Statute Book, anyone is tricked by words who imagines that Parliamentary government is still going on.

When the Socialist Government introduced direction of labour, Socialist speaker after speaker defended it on the argument that there was no real freedom of choice under capitalism and that capitalism was itself a form of direction of labour. Until then the electorate had been told that Socialism was going to be something better than pre-war capitalism. As time goes on, it comes increasingly to be defended by the Socialists with the argument that at any rate it is not any worse. But the important questions, before we decide whether it is better or worse, are: is it any different? And, if not, are both wrong or are both right?

This increase of the volume of Parliament's legislation and regulation went hand in hand with a strengthening of party discipline. As has been argued, Disraeli and Chamberlain imposed definite forms of organization on the Conservative and Liberal parties in the 1870's and 1880's. The parties might well have ossified in that latter decade had not a great issue arisen which broke down the newly built barriers of party loyalty—the issue of Home Rule for Ireland. On Home Rule men took their sides on what they saw as the intrinsic merit of the question irrespective of party loyalty. Chamberlain did not hesitate to break up the unity of the Liberal party, which he himself had done so much to build, and he and his friends crossed the floor of the House to form the Liberal-Unionist party. As a result over the next years the Conservatives and Liberal-Unionists were engaged on the delicate task of forging the new unity of the Unionist party. Such was clearly no moment for intensifying the rigidities of party discipline, and indeed Lord Salisbury, the Conservative leader of the day, was temperamentally unsuited for the mastership of a heresy-hunt. Unity having been achieved in opposition to Home Rule, the party was split once again on the new issue of Free Trade or Tariff Reform. Joseph Chamberlain, a man of radical temperament, found himself by an accident of opinion included within the Conservative party. Within the Conservative party he could never be a unifying force. He was bound to be a disruptive force. The Unionist party was by then under the weak leadership of Arthur Balfour. As a result, no coherent policy was imposed upon it. This was, it may be, greatly to the advantage of freedom of opinion, but it was to the disadvantage of the party, which provided an ineffective government until 1906 and then went down to humiliating defeat in the election of that year.

Meanwhile the Liberals, purged of the Liberal Unionists, who, apart from Chamberlain, were mainly of the old Whig faction, had their own difficulties. After Gladstone's retirement the leadership passed to Rosebery. Rosebery was an Imperialist whose enthusiasm for Irish Home Rule was at the best tepid. His traditions were of the Whig aristocracy, his habits scholarly and eccentric. He was but ill-suited to lead a party, which had been forced by circumstances to make Irish Home Rule the central point of its programme. He soon retired and went to plough his lonely furrow. But his retirement still left the party divided between the Imperialists—Asquith, Grey and Haldane—and the little Englanders—Campbell Bannerman, Lloyd George and Morley. The party was split over the Boer War, but divisions of opinion are less fatal to a party when it is in opposition than when it is in office. In spite of prophecies that it would be unable to do so, it was able to sink its differences and to form a coherent Government when the opportunity came to it in 1906.

The party system was in a curious state in the years between 1906 and 1914. The increased legislative programme inevitably involved a tightening of party discipline on both sides. Outwardly party politics had never been so bitter. The Irish question with its threat of civil war in particular aroused most deep feelings, and there was a sundering quality about party controversy such as had not been known in the days before English politics came to be dominated by Irish issues. Yet behind the scenes, as we know now, and behind the issues of Welsh Disestablishment or plural voting, by which the debates of Parliament were so easily filled, there was among leaders upon both sides grave apprehension both about the domestic and the international situation, anxious speculation whether the horizontal or the vertical catastrophe would come first. In such a situation and in spite of all the apparent bitterness of party controversy there were some leaders such as Mr. Lloyd George and Mr. Churchill who began to ask in private the question whether the day for party government had not passed and whether a national and all-party government was not required to guide the country through its troubles. Such obstinate questionings came immediately to nothing. The Government remained a purely Liberal Government up till 1914, but they certainly prepared the way and prepared opinion for the substitution of a Coalition Government for a party Government in 1915.

Thirty years and more have passed since this experiment was tried. People still repeat to one another the classic argument for party government. It is a strong argument. The argument is that, provided that both sides tacitly agree to respect the essential continuity of the nation's life, provided that controversy between them is confined to issues that are real indeed but secondary and the basically important issues are either left to other hands than those of the politicians or else settled by the politicians on non-party lines, then it is a great advantage to a nation that there should be two rival teams. The rule of neither of the teams would be wholly calamitous and between them the people can make their choice. A profound human instinct demands every now and again a change of rulers. It is the great

merit of Parliamentary government that it provides a
method by which this instinct for change can be satisfied
harmlessly, constitutionally and peacefully. In the days
when Mr. Belloc and Cecil Chesterton used to campaign
against the party system, they made it an accusation of
hypocrisy against the system that it greatly exaggerated the
differences between parties, but in reality that was clearly
its sovereign merit. Happy is the country where the politicians think that they differ from one another very profoundly,
where the people think that the politicians differ profoundly,
but where they do not in reality differ very much, so that
continuity of the national life is not upset by the one set
falling from power and the other succeeding to it.

Just as it is wise to give the people an opportunity of
changing the names of their rulers constitutionally, so in a
State where such an opportunity is not allowed, there is
obviously a great danger that they will change it un-
constitutionally—it may be for no deep reason but just
because, as Lamartine said in 1848, "France is bored".
"The best party", said Lord Halifax, the Trimmer, in
Charles II's reign, "is but a kind of conspiracy against the
rest of the nation." And Hertzen, the Russian thinker, in
the nineteenth century, divided the western world into
"on the one hand, the bourgeois proprietors who stubbornly
refuse to surrender their monopoly; on the other hand, the
bourgeois have-nots who want to wrest their property from
their hands but have no power to do so; that is to say,
on the one hand, avarice, and on the other, envy. Since
in actual fact no moral principle is involved in all this, the
position of any person on one side or the other is fixed by
the outward circumstances of his status and the position he
occupies in society. One of the opposing wolves fighting
the other gains the victory, that is to say, property or place,
and only passes over from the side of envy to the side of
avarice. Nothing could be more advantageous for this
transition than the fruitless exchanges of Parliamentary
debate. It gives movement and sets limits, it provides an
appearance of getting things done, and provides a setting

for the common interests, which is favourable to the attainment of its own personal ends." The first part of the quotation is vitiated by the excess of economic determinism, but the second is substantially fair. Had it not been for the accident of a personal quarrel between Asquith and Lloyd George in the middle of the last war—a quarrel that was in no way ideologically inevitable—there might well have never been an important Socialist party in this country. Had the Liberals fought the 1918 Election as a united party, they would have returned as at least the official opposition. The greater number of those who have found their spiritual home in the Socialist party would have found it comfortably enough in such a Liberal party, and the old game between Liberals and Conservatives might easily have gone on until this day.

But that has not happened, and now it is often said that the difference which divides the modern Socialist from the modern Conservative is a deeper difference than that which used to divide Liberal from Conservative in the old days. In a sense that is true. The difference between the dogmatic defender of *laissez-faire*, who would oppose any extension of State activity beyond that claimed by the Victorian State, and the dogmatic Socialist, who refuses to let any compromise stand in the way of the building of the classless society through nationalization, is indeed immense and a difference of principle and in kind, and the difference between the parties is often represented to be of that nature on the unreal battles of the platform. An academic Socialist may sincerely believe in the building of the classless society, but the real world of practical Socialists is far too busy in erecting a new class society to have much time to spare for these theoretical disquisitions.

On the other hand, on the Conservative side a few doughty champions may gallantly keep flying the flag of uncompromising individualism but their policy is by no means the policy of the Conservative party, nor is there any reason why it should be. It is a Conservative, not a reactionary, party, and the duty of a Conservative party is to conserve the essential institutions of the country. As such it is frankly and confessedly opportunist and accepts facts as they are, refusing to surrender itself like the doctrinaire Liberal or the doctrinaire Socialist to an abstract theory. The Conservative asks—and asks without shame or apology—not only how should industry be organized in some utopian, ideal society of the bloodless categories, but also what sort of solution are the men who in their various capacities have to work the industrial system here and now demanding. Statesmanship, especially in a democratic country, need not be ashamed to say, "This is the way the people want it done. That is in itself a reason for doing it this way, unless there are overwhelming reasons for believing that it is a way that would be for the country's disaster."

The consequence of all this is a curious paradox. So long as the differences between parties do not even pretend to be fundamental then party government can easily go on. Throughout the nineteenth century Liberals and Conservatives could alternate in power without any harm to the State, and few people wished it otherwise. There was no National Government and no demand for a National Government. When for a brief time, owing to the confusions over the split in the Tory party about the Repeal of the Corn Laws, there was a Coalition Government under Lord Aberdeen, it was neither popular nor effective. "England does not love coalitions", said Disraeli. It may be that he said it because he had not received office in that particular coalition, but it was certainly true.

Now in modern times it may still be true that England does not love coalitions. It probably is true, but for all that she has generally had them. People still enunciate their abstract, academic defence of party government. It is odd how rarely they seem to notice that in practice party government in modern times, whenever it is submitted to a strain, invariably breaks down. During the last thirty years we have spent twenty of them under some form or other of Coalition government and only ten under party government. I write at a moment when to prophesy is to

tempt the fates. A party Government is still at the moment
in power. The politicians of both parties proclaim their
abhorrence of a return to national government, and indeed,
though I claim no gift of prophecy, I do not think it probable
that we shall return to a National Government at least in
the sense in which that phrase was used in 1931—to a
Government in which the leaders of all the parties share out
the offices between themselves. For what is under criticism
is to-day not so much this political party or that political
party as the whole party system. The enthusiasm which
carried the Socialists to power has evaporated in face of
their patent and overwhelming incompetence. On the other
hand, there is no sign of a swing back to Conservatism.
The by-elections show no marked shift in the balance of
the parties. The political leaders content themselves with
saying that their opponents have no cure for the country's
troubles, and the public is all too well aware that the
Government has no solution and all too ready to believe
that the Opposition has not got one either. The great
danger is of a universal relapse into apathy and cynicism,
the danger that the country may be sinking into what
Matthew Arnold called "a prolonged death agony".

Now the first necessity is indeed to recognize the danger
of death of the party system as a fact. It is strange how little
this has been recognized. But having recognized it as a fact,
we must go on and inquire the reason. It is not that the
politicians of this generation are more lacking in courage,
or capacity, or principle than were their predecessors. I
know of no reason to believe that that is so. It is rather
that, when the nominal differences between the principles
of the two parties are very deep, then the party system
cannot work. National unity is unattainable and the
country slips down into anarchy and chaos. In all ages it
has always been a hateful evil to live in a divided society,
where neighbour feels himself at enmity with neighbour.
But in a primitive society such a life, if horrible, is at least not
impossible. It is not impossible for one self-supporting estate
to adhere to the Catholic religion and for the neighbouring

self-supporting estate to adhere to the Protestant religion, but in an industrial society there must be, if not a general agreement, at least a general acceptance of the system by which industry is to be organized. Otherwise all collapses into chaos. It is one of the problems of our complex, industrial system that a tiny minority, if only it occupies a few key positions, can prevent the carrying out of a national policy. Successful revolution in the modern world is almost impossible, but successful sabotage is easy.

It was this apparent lack of agreement which created the main problem of the inter-war and the post-war years. The very honesty of the disagreement accentuated the difficulty. An old-fashioned Conservative here and there might grumble that the Socialists were only a handful of agitators, who ought to be suppressed. An even more old-fashioned Socialist might complacently identify those of his own opinion with "the people" and mutter into his beard about "spivs and drones and vermin". But every sane man knew that both of these gentlemen were using their rhetoric to evade a very real dilemma. The dilemma was this. It was self-evident that what was needed was national unity. Yet how was national unity to be attained when half the nation honestly believed that industry should be ordered in one way and the other half believed that it should be ordered in another? The doctrinaire Socialist urged the Government to press ahead with its policy of nationalization, but whatever the other merits or demerits of nationalization, no one could pretend that it was uniting the nation. It was obviously dividing it more deeply. On the other hand, Conservative speakers who urged the Government to call off its nationalization programme for the sake of national unity were also perhaps a trifle ingenuous. This might please the enemies of nationalization, but would clearly disgust its friends. The nation would remain divided into its two camps, and all that would happen would be that the Government would change camps.

Formally the paradox appeared irreconcilable, but the true paradox was that the very depth of the division made it necessary to transcend it. On the nominal plane the problem must be settled by an apparent compromise. If one party wanted everything nationalized and the other party wanted nothing nationalized the obvious compromise was to nationalize some things and not to nationalize others. This was the nominal compromise but the real compromise was on a deeper plane. In the conflicts of real life victory goes not to the one protagonist nor to the other but on the Hegelian formula to some third force, and so it was in fact already obvious during the years when the Conservative or National Governments were in power that the day of capitalism, at any rate in the traditional sense of that word, had passed, and it was equally obvious as soon as the Socialists came into power that Socialism, at any rate in the sense of the classless society, was not destined to supplant it. While the politicians continue to tell us that the issue lies between capitalism and nationalization, with every day the capitalists are having less and less say in the industries that are left nominally to capitalism and the nation is having less and less say in the industries that are handed over nominally to nationalization. The ordinary shareholder does not buy shares in a company in order to control its policy any more than the ordinary Trade Unionist joins a Trade Union in order to control its policy. What both want is not power but irresponsibility. The Trade Unionist pays his Trade Union to look after the troubles of life for him. He does not want to pay and in addition have the bother of going to meetings. To do so would be to keep a dog and bark himself. In the same way, the investor wants a safe return on his money and no bother. The last thing that he wants is to be troubled with the control of a business that he does not understand. The shareholder neither interferes nor wishes to interfere with the working of his company, and, as the habit of financing out of reserves has grown, his very existence becomes increasingly irrelevant.

In the older and simpler days of the last century, if a man wished to build a factory, he could do so only on one of two conditions—on the condition either that he had the spare money to furnish his own capital or that he could persuade another man or other men to lend it to him. In the more complex world of to-day this is only true subject to very great reservation. The large firm, or combine, has its own ample financial reserves. If it wishes to build or buy a new factory, it can, if it likes, do so out of those reserves. It is of course true that, if it is going to pursue an expansive policy, it must sooner or later increase its capital. But it has a much larger freedom of choice of the moment when it makes that increase than had the old manufacturer. The raising of capital need no longer be related to a particular operation nearly as closely as it was a hundred years ago. Nor on the other hand—owing to the greater power of banks, to the growth of finance companies and investment trusts and middlemen of all sorts—is the investment made by the person who had made the saving nearly as frequently as it was a hundred years ago. As a result the investor does not to-day know what use is being made of his investment to anything like the extent that he did in the past, and this change renders many of the classical Ricardean arguments for the capitalist system no longer pertinent, and would equally do so if no such being as a Socialist had ever been heard of in the land.

The precise details of the shape of things to come no man can foresee. The general outlines of it are tolerably evident to all. The divorce between ownership and management has grown through the years through the evolution of events, not through the direct legislative enactments of either party. If industry is to produce the goods at all, then effective management must be concentrated in a few hands, over whom neither shareholders nor politicians can, because of their inevitable ignorance, exercise more than a very general and most nominal control, and, human nature being what it is, nothing can prevent those who have the power from using it to some extent to feather their own nests.

These are the realities of modern life, whatever the politicians on the one side or the other may see fit to pretend in their perorations. They are the realities of which all realists are aware. We can express them in the terms of Mr. Burnham's Managerial Revolution, or, if we prefer, we can express them in the terms used by Mr. Peter Drucker in his *End of Economic Man* and *Coming of Industrial Man.* If we use the latter phraseology, then we append to Mr. Burnham's thesis the important addendum that Mr. Burnham has shown how the managers are in fact coming to exercise power, but he has nothing to say on the all-important question whose solution is necessary if we are to enjoy a stable society —how to make the power of the managers legitimate— how to turn a *de facto* into a *de jure* authority. For, as Lord Hewart has truly said in his *New Despotism*, "Of all methods of administration that is the worst whereby real power is in the hands of one set of persons while public responsibility belongs to another set of persons".

CHAPTER V

LIBERTY IN THE NEW STATE

THE TRADE UNION is an instrument which has grown up within the capitalist society and which has a clear and useful function to perform within that society. It is the men's instrument for bargaining about wages and conditions of labour with the private employer. What function it should perform within a Socialist society, where the State is the employer, is a great deal less clear. It is of its nature essentially what may be called an instrument of opposition —what Peter Drucker calls an "anti" force—and, if the Socialist society were to become what the theoretical Socialist pretends that it is, a society in which the State in some Hegelian fashion expresses the mind of the citizen's true self—then there would be no legitimate place for a Trade Union as a body representing the workers and independent of the will of the State. In fact, of course, the workers have not under nationalization received at all that share of workers' control which they had been promised in the years of propaganda. They have received instead a mock-nationalization by which the power over, for instance, the mines has been handed over to managerial boards, which pretend to speak with the authority of the nation. The official Trade Union leaders, being politically associated with the Labour party, have pretended to recognize this trick-nationalization as a real nationalization and have attempted to persuade the workers that, since they are now working for the nation, it is their duty to refrain from strikes, and these strikes, since they are not sponsored by the Trade Unions, are dubbed unofficial. The effect of all that has sometimes been, it is true, to stop the strikes but at other times merely to ensure that the men now strike against their Trade Unions whereas previously they struck with them.

The effect of the Trade Unions' attempt to transform themselves from an organization of opposition into an organization of construction is merely to widen the gap, already dangerously wide, between the big Trade Union boss and the individual worker. Never was there a time when the Trade Unions were richer or had a larger membership than at present, but never also was there a time when their leaders had less moral authority. In the near future either the Trade Unions will have to reform themselves and find leaders who have a real moral authority over their followers, or alternatively the Trade Unions will go the way of the late mediaeval guilds and cease in any way to be representative of the workers. They will survive only as historical relics or as spokesmen of Government policy, and new instruments with new names will grow up who will speak for the workers in negotiations. That is, of course, the danger. We see it most clearly in the Transport and General Workers' Union—that vast, complex combine of a union. Its constitution is cumbersome and undemocratic. Its leaders, honest and admirable men, are indirectly elected and they have so entrenched themselves that their constitutional removal is difficult. What happens? The worker has given up in despair the attempt to reform his union constitutionally. He merely by-passes it and goes on strike in defiance of it and under leaders of his own when he wishes to do so. He no longer wastes his energy in trying to depose Mr. Deakin any more than he wastes his energy trying to depose the Garter-King-of-Arms, for the one matters to him no more than the other.

So, too, with the political Socialists, who are to so large an extent the same people as the Trade Union leaders. Just like the individualists of the school of Sir Waldron Smithers, they are men living in a past age. Socialism is essentially a creed of the age of capitalism. It makes sense as a criticism of capitalism, but it no longer makes sense in a world in which capitalism is already, for reasons quite irrelevant to the Socialist criticism, passing away. The Bolsheviks in 1917, being old men whose minds had been formed in the Victorian age, naturally attacked the problem in an old-fashioned way and began by nationalizing all the means of production and distribution. But the Nazis of a later date were able to see that ownership was no longer the point of importance. They by-passed the problem of nationalization. They allowed the owners of industry to remain nominal owners, but controlled their policy and controlled their profits. So did the British National Government during the war though their controls were less drastic and less violent, and, what between the degree of control of profits and policy envisaged by the Conservatives in their industrial schemes and the degree of incentive which the Socialists will have to concede in order to get the goods produced, the difference between the two parties on that point, though real, is not nearly as large as it is the fashion to pretend.

There is an overwhelmingly strong argument against nationalizing an industry that is at the moment working satisfactorily, such as for instance iron and steel—an argument that is not theoretical but pragmatic. It is obviously the height of folly to disturb such an industry, the more particularly at such a time as this. The more it is true that the new system is merely going to be the old system dolled up afresh, the greater the folly of upsetting everybody to make the unnecessary change. There is an especial folly in swopping horses in mid-stream when each horse is the twin brother of the other.

But such controversies neglect the real issue. The real issue is this. We are moving, whatever the political complexion of our Government, into an age where a large and probably an increasing proportion of our industry will be concentrated in large units, and these large units can only produce efficiently if great authority is vested in management. Is it possible to make that managerial power legitimate? Will the political power be able to control the managerial power or will the managerial power be completely irresponsible?

In answer to the second question we are told that in the

dictatorial State, whatever the power conceded to the managers, yet the political power—Stalin and Hitler—remains and remained the final master.

This is perhaps true, but there are three answers. In the first place, we are at present only at the beginning of the managerial revolution. It is yet to be seen where final victory will lie. Dallin in *The Real Soviet Russia* notes not so much the present dominance as the growing power of the managers. Secondly, the theory of the managerial revolution obviously only makes an assertion about what must be done if a society is to solve its problems and to produce its goods. Neither Russia nor Hitlerite Germany has solved its problems. Such evidence as that, for instance, of Kravchenko's *I Chose Freedom* shows that, though more than thirty years had been allowed them for preparation—years during which according to their own boast they had not allowed bourgeois illusion to lull them into any false security about the intention of the non-Communist world to attack them—the Bolsheviks were taken by the German attack in a state of total unpreparedness and chaos. They were only able to survive, in spite of overwhelming odds in their favour and in spite of enormous losses, owing to the happy accident that there were two great capitalist societies which could actually supply them with the goods. Rather like Great Britain under the Socialist Government and in the days of the American loan, the planned society was just able to survive owing to the existence of the unplanned societies which actually provided it with the goods. Hitlerite Germany did, it is true, actually produce goods—and it is also true that within Hitlerite Germany Hitler was the master and Schacht was the servant. Yet Hitlerite Germany has fallen. It produced goods, but it did not produce sufficient goods to sustain its own lunatic policy, and it is at least arguable that Germany would have fared better if she had allowed herself to be ruled by a manager rather than by a megalomaniac.

Yet, whatever the true lessons to be drawn from the experiences of Russia and Germany, they are lessons that are irrelevant to our inquiry of the moment. It is arguable that a dictator is strong enough to stand up to the managers. But is a party Parliamentary minister strong enough to stand up to them? That is a wholly different question. It is clear that a dictator is at a very great advantage over a Parliamentary politician in such a conflict. The dictator is theoretically irremovable. He stands for a continuous policy just as much as do the managers. But the Parliamentary minister is of his very nature transient—here to-day and gone to-morrow. Now, whatever else may be debatable, it is not debatable that a great industry requires continuity of policy if it is to survive. Decisions have to be made about capital expenditure, which is only expected to bear its fruits some years ahead. All will be thrown into chaos if there are constant changes of policy. Therefore the country cannot go on at all, if the periodical changes of ministers and parties in power bring with them constant changes of industrial policy. Industrial policy must in fact be kept out of party politics, whether the nominal responsibility lies with the political minister or not. This means that the more nominal responsibility is piled upon the shoulders of politicians, the more necessary is it that they should not in fact exercise that responsibility. The more that the Socialists clamour that the state should run industry, the more certain do they make it that in fact industry will run the state—that, or, as I say, the collapse into chaos.

It is this overriding need for continuity in industrial policy which makes it certain that in a tug of wills the irremovable managers will defeat the removable ministers. "The acceptance of a planned economy", writes Professor Laski in *Reflections on the Revolution of Our Time*, "involved the necessity to think of freedom in terms of the assumption that the decision to plan is broadly respected...Freedom will not be maintained if there is room for doubt whether the decision to plan as an essential element of its life is likely to be reversed by some chance hazard of electoral fortunes." It does not greatly matter how the authority may be divided between the minister and the managerial

board in the relevant nationalizing Act. Those who bother
very greatly about the particular provisions of these acts
in my opinion a little waste their time. These issues are
settled by realities, not by clauses in an Act of Parliament.

Now it is easy enough to argue from all this that there is
no room for freedom in the modern industrial state, that
Parliament, if it survives at all, can only survive, as is the
attractive English habit, as a relic. For here, instead of
violently destroying our institutions as they do in other
countries when they have outlived their usefulness, we preserve the formalities and pageantry but strip them of their
real power. Just as the monarchy and the House of Lords
in a sense survive, so there is no reason why six hundred odd
ladies and gentlemen should not go through some ancient
ritual from time to time of standing-up and bowing to the
Speaker but there is no longer, one might argue, any
possibility that they will govern the country. In the years
after the last war that uneven genius, Oswald Spengler,
was already prophesying "With the beginning of the
twentieth century Parliamentarism (even English) is tending
rapidly towards taking upon itself the role that it once
assigned to the Kingship. It is becoming an impressive
spectacle for the multitude of the orthodox, while the
centre of gravity of big policy, already *de jure* transferred
from the crown to the people's representatives, is passing
de facto from the latter to unofficial groups and the will
of unofficial personages. The World War"—that is the first
World War—"almost completed this development. There
is no way back to the old Parliamentarism from the domina-
tion of Lloyd George and the Napoleonism of the French
militarists." On the contrary, the movement has clearly
gone forward, while Parliamentary control has become but
a pretence. Mr. Amery in his *Thoughts on the Constitution*,
quarrels with Bagehot for his assertion that in this country
we have Parliamentary government. Our Government,
Mr. Amery argues, is a Cabinet Government. But may it
not be that in Bagehot's time, with Parliament still in
possession of its freedom we had Parliamentary government,

that to-day in Mr. Amery's time we have Cabinet government, but that soon we shall have neither Parliamentary
government nor Cabinet government, but that power will
pass wholly out of the hands of those nominally responsible
for it, and we shall have managerial government?

It is clearly very easy to propound an argument, clothed
in every appearance of logic, that the developments of
modern industrialism demand a live society in which there
is no room for liberty and that the death of liberty is inevitable. Those who most vigorously deny the inevitability
of the death of liberty must be the first, as they look around
on the other countries of the world and as they look at many
of the tendencies of this country, to admit the possibility
of its death. No one who remembers the world as it was
before 1914 and remembers what was taken for granted in
that world and contrasts that with what has actually happened over the last thirty years, can feel any easy confidence
that liberty—or indeed any of the other values which we
have hitherto considered to be the marks of a civilized
man—will inevitably survive. Nor is it very likely to survive
unless it is defended for its own sake and as a spiritual value
necessary in itself

We, as Professor Jung would put it—we of the West—
are of a certain nature. Western man has not always had
freedom and justice but he has always wanted them. He
can live for a time without the reality but he cannot live
without the vision. The problem of liberty in the modern
world is self-evidently a difficult problem. But first it is
not a problem that we can solve or leave unsolved at whim.
We must solve it or we cannot live at all.

The problem before the modern statesmen is then—how
can we find a place for freedom in this new managerial
world? The honourable and gallant skirmisher of the
rearguard fight who invokes precedent from the past to
condemn every new encroachment of the Executive and
appeals back to the traditions of the constitution is within its
limits to be applauded and encouraged. Yet he fights with
an exposed flank and he is vulnerable. It is always open to

the encroacher to reply, "These liberties were tolerated
when the Government did much less than it does to-day.
But if the Government is going to have all these increased
responsibilities, it cannot perform them unless it has the
requisite power." And this indeed is true. Unless we have
a radical reform of the whole scheme of the constitution,
then it is certain that the future lies with tyranny. A breakdown of the present compromise will be merely a prelude
to inevitable tyranny. The argument is irresistible.
"Because we had respect for the traditions and prejudices
of the English people", its champions will say, "therefore
we attempted to combine a planned society with the
preservation of traditional English freedom. But we were
well aware from the first of the incompatibility of the two
conceptions. The breakdown has proved that we cannot
have the two together. Therefore, having proved our good
will by our honest attempts, we must now go ahead and
build the planned society, without regard to freedom."

Parliamentary government has already very largely
perished. The member is the obedient servant of the party
machine. He tramps into the division lobby voting for or
against he knows not what on subjects upon which as a
general rule no opinion save that of the specialist is of the
least value. The matters which were the subject of legislation
in Victorian days were matters upon which any educated
man could form an opinion. On these bills for the reorganization of industry no one can have an opinion of the
least value unless he happens to have had personal experience of the industry in question. A dozen or more
of members may have had that experience. They sit through
the afternoon and make the speeches of the debate. Such
experience may perhaps give reality to the debates, but,
when it comes to the division, those with knowledge are on
each issue hopelessly out-numbered by the ignorant. As
things are now, it would really be simpler and more
economical to keep a flock of tame sheep and from time to
time to drive them through the division lobbies in the appropriate numbers. Absurd and excessive hours of meeting,

constant all-night sittings, do not prove, as is sometimes superficially claimed, that Parliament is working hard; they prove that Parliament is not working at all. If the legislature was really legislating, if the shape of the laws was really in the least influenced by the debates and votes of members of Parliament, then it is clear that no one would dream of asking them to hold their debates under such ridiculous conditions. Who would dream of taking the advice of his solicitor or his banker at half-past-five in the morning after having kept him up all night?

When I served on the Lord Chancellor's Committee for the reform of County Court Procedure, it greatly struck me that everyone at once and very sensibly agreed that it would be very foolish to extend the judges' hours of sitting, because, it was argued, if judges sit too long, they will give foolish judgements. This argument was accepted because it mattered what judges say. But it obviously does not matter what members of Parliament say. Members of Parliament are allowed to give their opinions under such ridiculous conditions only because the Government has already made up its mind that it is not going to pay attention to those opinions in any event. The formality of debate is tolerated, and from time to time the sleepers are awakened and driven through the division lobby in support of they know not what. The decisions have all been taken elsewhere and beforehand. The private member can still indeed do humble work of very high importance by bringing the grievances of individual constituents to the notice of the appropriate minister, and this work is more important than ever it was with the vastly extended range of Government activity, but it is work that could be done just as well if no such thing as a Chamber existed. The anxious constituent sometimes asks his member, "Will you raise this matter in the House?" But a great deal more often than not to raise a grievance in the House is the very worst way of getting it remedied. The minister and his department are on their dignity under public fire. They are reluctant to admit to a mistake. A private letter will often find them a great deal more amenable.

Within the House the freedom of the vote has gone save on the rarest occasions. Private members' time went for the war—in theory, temporarily and for the crisis. A pittance of it has been returned, but what likelihood is there of ever seeing any private members' bills on the statute book? Who has ever heard of crises coming to an end, whatever may be the demands of etymology, in a modern totalitarian State? Legislation is coming to be increasingly delegated legislation and even legislation by delegation of delegation. A minister issues a notice under the authority of an order. Parliament can take no cognizance of the notice. On another occasion he does not even issue a public notice and citizens are held to obedience to regulations of which they could not in any possible way have heard. Against the order members can "pray" but their prayers are automatically voted down by the massed battalions. They can raise on the adjournment such matters as are not matters of legislation, and a tired minister will reply to them and there may be two or three other members scattered about the benches. It may advantage a member with his constituents to be able to point to the evidence of his adjournment to prove that he is alive to some local grievance, but it is a little difficult to see what further purpose it serves. Service on the Committee of Estimates or the Committee on Public Expenditure is almost the only truly valuable form of service still open to the private member.

There remains only Question Time and it will be interesting indeed to see whether that privilege of private members survives intact. Already ministers reply to the curiosity of their questioners by refusing to disclose details of the policy of the Managerial Boards which govern our great industries. Mr. Herbert Morrison frankly tells the House that it will not be given information on the day-to-day decisions of nationalized industries. By an odd paradox, members can ask questions about non-nationalized industries and cannot ask them about nationalized industries. At a date after the appointed day for the nationalization of the railways but before the appointed day for the nationalization of road transport, a number of my constituents were stranded one Saturday night in Bath and could not get home to Devizes. I found that I could ask the Minister of Transport why an extra bus could not be put on for them and receive a courteous reply because road transport had not been nationalized, but I could not ask the Minister why an extra train could not be put on for them because railways had been nationalized.

It will be very interesting to see whether in the near future there are still further restrictions on questions of that sort, and, it may be, on all questions. If such restrictions should come, they will not come out of any personal passion for tyranny by the ministers. All that the minister has to do at Question Time is to read out a sentence or two from a typewritten sheet. It is doubtless a bore but it is no very onerous task. It is from the managers that the demand for the restrictions on Parliamentary freedom will come. The members of the managerial boards will say that it is impossible for them to take responsibility for the management of a great industry, if their policy is to be subject at any time to inconvenient publicity through question and answer between a private member and a minister, neither of whom in all probability really understands what is at issue. A business can only be run if a good deal of information is kept confidential and persons of competence will make their protection the condition of their acceptance of the managerial positions.

And yet, it if be necessary to provide the managers with sufficient freedom and authority for them to perform their functions, it is equally necessary to see to it that their power is not irresponsible. Man cannot bear irresponsible power and remain sane, as so many thousand clamorous instances of history record. "Absolute power", Lord Acton told us, "tends to corrupt absolutely", and this—it is most important to remember—is not merely true of moral corruption but almost more of intellectual corruption. Men stop thinking when they no longer have the stimulus of criticism. The common Socialist criticism says that capitalist society is

in any event moving towards monopoly. Mr. Peter Drucker
has shown that it is indeed moving towards large units
but that in most industries it is moving towards two or
three units rather than towards a single unit—simply
because intelligent capitalism has come to understand that
it must preserve a minimum of competition if it is to retain
that efficiency that is necessary to keep it up to the mark
and to ensure its own survival. Now under the capitalist
system the State did not attempt to control the capitalist
directly. He was left free to do what he would with his own
—subject only to the not very onerous condition that he
keep within the bounds of the criminal law. But the check
on him was that he operated with his own money. If he
behaved foolishly, he lost his money. Critics of the system
may say that there was far from an inevitable coincidence
between conduct that was socially desirable and conduct that
was financially profitable. Defenders of the system may claim
that under it and as a result of it the standard of living of the
people, and above all the standard of living of the poor,
increased incomparably more than it had increased in all
previous recorded history. The impartial observer notes
that the system has in any event passed away.

With none of these arguments are we at the moment
concerned. The question is rather—what will be the check
on the managers under the new system? They are not
operating with their own money. So long as Government
subsidies persist, the managers of an industry may not even
have the collective responsibility of making their industry
self-supporting. Incompetence will not hit them in their
own pockets—short, of course, of such overwhelming and
universal incompetence as to upset the whole system—
and our purpose is to find a way by which the individual
can be punished, exposed and extruded before a general
spread of incompetence has upset the whole system, just as
he was punished, exposed and extruded by bankruptcy in the
old system. The control of the Parliamentary politician
cannot possibly prove more than a legal fiction; the control
of the dictator would be a remedy worse than the disease.

CHAPTER VI

THE REFORM OF PARLIAMENT

WHERE CAN we find a remedy? Can we find it in a reform of the present Parliamentary constitution? It is clear that Parliamentary government to-day is rapidly breaking down. There are two reasons which cause the breakdown of institutions. They break down because they are in themselves no longer suited to the needs of the age, and they break down because they are no longer able to attract to their service people of ability and integrity. The latter is a much more common cause of breakdown than is commonly understood. Shallow reformers often assume that, whatever the conditions that they impose, the supply of worthy recruits for every one of the great professions will still be adequate. They make no allowance for the very rapid fluctuations in the prestige of professions. For instance, there is most grave danger that Mr. Bevan's health scheme will collapse because it has imposed conditions under which for the future men of ability will not consent to become doctors. Is there danger of a similar famine in the political world?

If we ask the question why anybody ever goes into Parliament at all, the question is by no means a simple one. The disamenities and disadvantages of the.life are manifold and manifest. The member of Parliament is at the beck and call of all men day after day from eight o'clock in the morning until twelve o'clock at night. The problems pour in upon him thick and fast without respite and from all directions. He has to give so many decisions that he can never properly give his mind to anything. He has to sacrifice his home life, his recreations and even that cultural background from which we may presume his political convictions derived and without refreshment from which all political convictions must become arid and tasteless and mechanically repetitive. Very few members of Parliament in my experience read many books after their election to Parliament. In return what does he get? In Parliament he finds an unhealthy life full of temptations, all the frustration of endless hours of bobbing up and down to catch the Speaker's eye in order in the end to mumble for a quarter of an hour to empty benches. Supposing that he has something to say, there could not well be any place where the saying of it is less likely to have effect than in the House of Commons. On the wireless he can reach millions, in the newspapers hundred of thousands, where in the House of Commons he reaches perhaps twenty of whom the majority probably are not listening. He has to play his part in the party game, much of which the keenest of politicians must with all the will in the world often feel to be a dreary and childish farce. A few persons of a certain temperament prefer to live their lives and to do their talking thus in the public gaze, but to the normal man it is an unnatural life—the life of a man living continually on his nerves. He, alone, is never able to put his business from his mind. Other men when they go home or go out to dinner, are able—are indeed compelled—to talk of other things than their business. The politician can never do so. Every person who sits next to him at a table always asks him about politics. "When are you going to get them out, Mr. X? Will there be a war, Mr. X? Will they abolish petrol rationing, Mr. X?" The topics pursue him even into his home.

What is it that causes anyone to lead such a life?

Politicians are not all of a piece, any more than other people. Every sort of motive from the highest ideal of disinterested service to the lowest and most sordid self-seeking leads men to politics, and most politicians, being of the human way, are doubtless led by a mixture of motives that are a little bit below the highest and a little bit above the lowest. But, if we were to assume that the motive of all politicians was one of a pure desire for service, we still should not have found an answer to our question why men become politicians. Why does anyone choose to serve in that way rather than other ways?

The most common answer is that politicians are driven by the love of power, and this is an answer which is sensible as far as it goes and which also suits well with the fashions of modern psychology. For modern psychologists, like Adler, have justly criticized the insufficiency of the capitalist and socialist economists of the nineteenth century, who taught that man was always moved by his economic advantage. Wealth, Adler has taught, is only one form of power, and it is power rather than wealth which is the ruling human motive, and certainly it is the love of power rather than the love of wealth which is the motive which drives men to politics.

But, if we are told that power is the politicians' motive, that again is in danger of being an insufficient explanation unless indeed we examine very closely what we mean by power and give it a wider connotation than it would seem at first sight to bear. Obviously the number of politicians who have any significant share in shaping the destiny of nations is very small. Of three or four members of a Cabinet, at most, could this be said—in many Cabinets of one only—in some Cabinets of none. The vast majority of members of Parliament not only do not have power in that sense at any given moment but do not ever have it, and indeed of most it is obvious from their first entry that there is no serious possibility of their ever attaining the positions of power. Of the six hundred odd members of Parliament there cannot be much more than a score or so who are even seriously competing for the highest posts.

For the rest, the prospect before them, whether on Government bench or on Opposition bench, whether in minor office or out of it, is that, far from taking decisions themselves, they must live a life in which it is peculiarly apparent to them that the decisions are taken by other people. The man in the street may think that the ordinary member of Parliament is an important person and has power. The member of Parliament himself cannot possibly think so.

What is the motive other than the motive of pure service that keeps the ordinary member in politics? The first answer is, I think, this. The under-secretary and the minister, who does not hold one of the three or four top posts, has indeed little power but he has a good deal of consideration. He sits at the heads of tables. He has a carpet in his room. There is an appearance of deferring to him—and indeed even the ordinary member of Parliament, who is not a minister, gets a certain amount of verbal consideration. There is no doubt that to some people consideration is a substitute for power and some people indeed even prefer the appearance of power to the responsibility of its reality. People are pleased not so much by what they are as by what other people think that they are.

This is harmless enough, if a little silly. But it must in honesty be confessed that there is another less pleasant motive which drives some people on through their political career. More common than the positive love of getting jobs is the negative hatred of other people getting them. There are beyond question people who are kept in politics not so much because they want to be famous themselves as because they cannot bear the thought that others, junior and less distinguished, will be more famous than they. On certain souls there rests—we know not why—a curse, a gnawing ambition which will not let them be and take the world as they find it, and owing to which they cannot bear to leave the world without their mark upon it. This spiritual restlessness is by far the greatest misfortune that can fall upon a man and we must pity those who suffer from it. But it is clearly a peculiar evil of so-called democratic constitutions—of constitutions where career is open to what are ironically called the talents.

What brings a man to the top is not superior ability but—much more often—an intense desire for success, that extra little ounce of ambition that is not quite sane. Plato said that no one should have power except the man who did not wish to have it. This is a counsel of perfection, but at least

it is a great merit of semi-aristocratic constitutions that the
ambitious man is balanced by a Hartington or a Salisbury
who hates power but who holds it simply because he is
compelled to hold it by the accident of his birth. How are
we going to keep the balance against ambition in our new
constitution? We cannot hope to do it unless we find a way
of substituting true self-government for the present pseudo-
self-government. Charlatans always flourish and are bound
to flourish in institutions which are themselves a fraud. For
Parliament is at present losing prestige for two reasons—
first, because it has not discovered a way of solving the
industrial problem—second, because new methods of
communication have of their nature lessened the importance
of representative institutions. No State, thought Aristotle,
could be a good State where all the citizens could not at the
same time hear the voice of one man, and representation
was a compromise—the nearest approach that was possible
to self-government if you were to have a State too large to
be reached by the single voice. "The English people",
thought Rousseau, "is only free once in seven years—on the
day of a General Election."

The Parliamentary debate had its transcendent importance
in the eighteenth and early nineteenth centuries because
Parliament was the only place where the nation's leaders
made their statements of policy. In mid-Victorian times
Chamberlain, Bright, and, above all, Gladstone, adopted
what was then the new habit of speaking direct to the people
in large public meetings, but physical limitations still
prevented the majority of people from hearing them or any
individual from hearing them very often. The unaided voice
can only reach to a comparatively small audience. The
Parliamentary debate maintained its predominance.

The years after the 1914 war saw a great growth in
politicians' journalism, and the politician could reach a
much larger audience by his pen than he could by the spoken
word. As a result, we saw a decline in the importance of
the Parliamentary debate, and, even at a time when paper
was not yet scarce, Parliamentary debates ceased to be

reported in the press as fully as they had been in the last century. At the beginning of the last century *The Times* consisted of two pages of which one was devoted to the Parliamentary report. Yet, for all its disadvantages, the spoken word could make a personal appeal that the written word could never emulate, and, as long as it had only the competition of journalism and literature to fear, Parliament's predominance would probably have remained unshaken. But the modern inventions of the amplifier and the microphone have changed the nature of the challenge. Thanks to the amplifier the modern statesman can address tens of thousands if only he can persuade them to come to listen to him. Thanks to the microphone he can address millions, who do not even have to make a journey. The modern statesman can speak directly to the nation as his predecessor could not. We are back to Aristotle in a way that Aristotle could not have guessed. Statesmen, with a few exceptions, have perhaps been curiously slow to understand the profound political revolution which the invention of broadcasting makes inevitable. But they are coming to understand it now—to understand how the direct speech on the wireless is a thousand times more important than the Parliamentary debate, and, if Parliament does not show itself capable of performing an essential function in the modern world, it is inevitable that people will ask with ever-increasing insistence, "Is the clumsy, indirect device of representative institutions any longer necessary?"

If we look to the political uses to which broadcasting has so often been put in other countries, we cannot be blind to the enormous danger if that question should be asked by impatient men and women. But things are as they are. We do not avoid the danger by denying it. We cannot hope to survive through a political technique which was essentially formed by, and suited to, the conditions of the eighteenth century. We must face the fact that we have passed into an age that is no longer an age in which Parliamentarians can live by mutual congratulation—an age in which Parliament can only survive if it justifies itself.

On the other hand, representative institutions are menaced to-day from the opposite direction by the Gallup poll. "In the old days", we are told, "it was necessary to allow representatives to act as spokesmen for public opinion. Now we have discovered a scientific way of ascertaining what public opinion is. Is there any further need for representatives?" The election of President Truman has fortunately answered that question.

It may well be argued from the experiments of Switzerland, Australia and other countries that there is a type of question—such as, for instance, Sunday cinemas—that is both simple and unrelated to general policy and which can usefully perhaps be settled by a plebiscite. But this is very far from true of all questions. Most important questions can only be solved as a part of a general coherent policy. If we wish to demand by ultimatum certain concessions from Patagonia, then we must adopt a whole pattern of military, of foreign, of industrial policy, without which we should be in no position to carry our demands on Patagonia to success. Now the voter in the Gallup poll, receiving a sudden call from the canvasser in the middle of cooking the Sunday dinner, is asked, "Should we stand up to Patagonia?" She has had no opportunity of saying whether a policy should hitherto have been pursued or whether a policy has hitherto been pursued which makes it possible for us to stand up to Patagonia. She cannot know what would be the repercussions on our relations with other Powers, on our industrial situation at home—if we were to stand up to Patagonia. Similarly, if the Gallup voter is asked, "Should we nationalize the mines?" What do you mean by nationalization? There are a variety of different schemes. Would the miners accept it? Who is going to provide the capital under the new scheme? What will be the effect on the price of coal? What margin for rising prices have we if we are to keep our export markets? What are likely to be the terms of trade in the coming years? To all these questions the Gallup voter must know the answer if she is to cast an intelligent vote. But how often does she know them?

For these reasons it would be indeed a folly if we were to allow Gallup polls to establish themselves as substitutes for Parliamentary responsibility. But they are more than an irrelevance; they are a danger. They are a danger because, under democracy as under any other system, no country can prosper, no policy can be carried through to success, unless the country has leaders who are prepared on occasion and in detail to do unpopular things. The danger of politicians misrepresenting their electorates to-day is not great. Politicians have their ears much too close to the ground for that. The danger of politicians not having the courage on occasion to defy their electorates is very much greater. The modern politician is often indecently sensitive to the risk of losing a few votes and any device that is likely to increase his natural timidity is a device against the public interest. People who challenge the doctrine of Burke and argue that a member of Parliament should be not a representative but a delegate do not, I think, wholly understand what they are saying. A man may go to a particular conference, armed with instructions, and vote not in accordance with his own judgement but as those who sent him ordered. But Parliament is not a particular conference; it is a way of life. That any man could ever consent to barter away his judgement and to sit in an assembly, day in day out, voting not according to his own opinion but at the instruction of others is unthinkable. The only result of such a theory would be that no man of integrity would submit himself to the humiliation of sitting in such an assembly. It would inevitably destroy the last relic of sincerity in the Parliamentary debate, as the member would go to the debate, pledged by his instructions how to vote before ever he had heard any of the arguments. Things, we are often told, are bad enough now owing to excessive party discipline. They would be a hundred times worse under a theory of delegation.

How then can we reform Parliament to make it competent of solving its modern problems?

There are, of course, a variety of schemes for the reform

of the method of election to the House of Commons. Proportional representation has its advocates. Proportional representation claims that it gives a mathematically more accurate representation of the electorate. It is designed to give, and presumably would give, greater representation to smaller parties. But whether this would be desirable is far more open to question. It can well be argued that it was proportional representation that was responsible for putting Hitler into power in Germany. The great advantage of the two-party system, alongside of all its self-evident absurdities, is that under it it is mathematically certain that it will at all times be possible to obtain a Government that has the support of the majority of the House. It thus assures a reasonable stability of Government, and, although at any particular election the winning party is always over-represented and the losing party under-represented, yet it may be argued that over the term of elections these unfair advantages cancel one another out and that therefore the representation over the whole is not unfair.

Yet at the same time it must be admitted that the defence of the two-party system as advanced by the official apologists of the two major parties is a trifle comic. A one-party system and a three-party system are to them alike anathema. But, if it is an insult to ask a free man to live in a State where he is not allowed to express any opinion save that dictated to him by one party which he may dislike, it is surely only less of an insult to ask him to live in a State where he is not allowed to express any opinion save those dictated to him by one of two parties, both of which, it may equally be, he dislikes.

There are, it is certainly true, solid advantages in having the membership of Parliament substantially divided between two parties, but it is questionable whether these advantages are so large as to justify the maintenance of an unfair electoral system simply in order that the parties may be confined to two. There are solid arguments against proportional representation. Party considerations apart, it is a great virtue in the present system that every elector

knows that there is one member of Parliament who is his
member and on whose services he has a right to call for a
remedy of his grievances. This advantage would be lost if
large five—or seven—member constituencies were substituted for the present arrangement. On the other hand, if we
reject proportional representation, there seems no sufficient
reason for rejecting the alternative vote. Whether the
introduction of the alternative vote would in fact help the
Liberals and other small parties as much as they think, it
would be interesting to see. At the 1945 election by far the
greater number of Liberals were at the bottom of the poll
on the first count and would therefore have been eliminated
under the alternative vote. It is doubtful if its existence
would have made much difference to the result, but at least
it would have deprived two million people of a certain sense
of grievance.

Yet, whatever the rights about these reforms of electoral
methods, they clearly do not touch the real problem which
is that Parliamentary government is to-day breaking down
because Parliament has neither the time nor the competence
to perform the tasks allotted to it. Another suggested line
of remedy is that of devolution—the concession of local
Home Rule to the various parts of the island. This was the
alternative to Gladstone's Irish Home Rule which was put
forward by Joseph Chamberlain. "Set up a whole series of
local Parliaments", said Chamberlain, "of which the Irish
can be one." Certainly if one reckons up the proportion of
Parliamentary time that was devoted to Irish issues before
1914 and the additional tasks that have been piled upon
Parliament's shoulders since 1914, it is impossible to resist
the conclusion that, had Irish self-government not been
achieved, English self-government could never have survived.
It is the Irish Free State which has saved the British Parliamentary system. Yet it was unrealistic to think that the
Irish question could have been solved by treating it as a
mere part of a general question of devolution and it is
equally unrealistic to think that devolution could be a
solution of the modern problem of the overloading of

Parliament. The great argument for having a separate Irish legislature was that in any event you had separate Irish legislation—that the problems of Ireland were in any event different from the problems of Great Britain, that laws applicable to Ireland usually were not applicable to Great Britain and that laws applicable to Great Britain usually were not applicable to Ireland.

Therefore the concession of Home Rule to Ireland has been an enormous relief to the legislative machinery at Westminster, but it cannot be pretended that a concession of Home Rule to Scotland or Wales would have at all a comparable effect. There may be a great deal to be said for such devolution of authority on its intrinsic merits, but it would not sensibly lighten the burden at Westminster. The amount of time devoted to purely Welsh affairs is almost negligible. Scotland, it is true, has her own days and her own Bills, but the Bills usually follow very closely the lines of the parallel English Bill. The truth is that Scotland and Wales have been integrated into the general British industrial system, as Ireland never was. The great industrial problems must be dealt with as a whole by the central machinery. There cannot be separate solutions for Scotland and Wales from those for England, although of course there is both room and need for flexibility in detail of administration to meet local conditions. Wales and Scotland certainly enrich the present House of Commons because there alone is local feeling strong enough to insist on the election of local members. Elsewhere the effect of territorial constituencies based on no strong territorial feeling is that the same sort of member tends to be returned by all constituencies. All members represent, and devote themselves to the attempt to satisfy, the numerically predominant class, the working class, an admirable class but not the whole of society and a class dependent even for its own well-being on the well-being of other classes.

The Marxians tell us that labour is the sole producer of wealth. It is a falsehood, and a dangerous falsehood, precisely because of its superficial appearance of truth.

There is no danger of anyone believing that all wealth was produced by poets or clergymen or company directors, but it is just possible that a stupid person would believe that all wealth was produced by manual labour. It is not in any party spirit that I call attention to this danger. The protest is not a mere Conservative protest against a temporary Socialist predominance. On the contrary, from a purely party point of view it is very uncertain to whose advantage the present unbalance will prove. It is certain that, if this present constitution survives, then party divisions will show themselves within it. No one can imagine that the working-class will permanently give an undivided allegiance to the present Socialist party simply because it calls itself Labour. Party divisions will certainly re-emerge, whatever the precise lines along which they run, and in all probability there will again be a Conservative Government, since Conservatism is one of the enduring demands of mankind. But the Conservative party has endured throughout the generations, while other parties have come and gone, precisely because, unlike other parties, it has never been tied to a particular class or a particular form of society but has stood rather for the conservative mood—for the preservation of the order and balance of the society which it found in existence. Thus there was a conservatism of monarchy, which under Bolingbroke fought a Jacobite fight for the preservation of a real power of the crown, at the beginning of the eighteenth century. There was a Tory party which fought a similar battle though for a different monarch under George III. Then under Pitt came the Toryism of the aristocratic society which opposed the Jacobinism of the French Revolution. With the Whig victory of the Reform Bill men glibly prophesied that the Tory party was dead but Peel by his Tamworth Manifesto built up a Toryism of the manufacturer and the middle class, and to-day there is little doubt that a new Conservatism of the working-class will emerge, probably bearing that name and certainly expressing that philosophy.

There is certainly no more profoundly conservative class

in this country than the working-class and a Conservative
working-class party will in many ways be an admirable
party. But it does not solve; it accentuates the particular
difficulty that we are at the moment considering. The danger
is that territorial democracy will in the future give us not
only one but two parties that are both predominantly of
the wage-earning class. A new Tory democracy will emerge,
will challenge and will doubtless in the end challenge
successfully the doctrinaire Socialists. It will be its task to
defend the freedom of the working-class against the excessive
power of the managerial class which Socialism is bringing
into being. That is a noble task, in which we must wish
them well. Yet the solution lies not in a new form of class-
consciousness, but in the transcendence of class-consciousness.
That is only possible first, when there is a tolerable solution
of the economic problem and a wide distribution of property,
secondly, when there is the acceptance of a general philosophy
which teaches that there are other things more important
than economics.

Therefore there is no solution in devolution. The solution
must be found in readjusting the burden at the centre.
There are some who would reform the House of Lords. The
House of Lords is to-day a hereditary chamber in hardly
more than name. By far the greater burden in its debates
are born by distinguished statesmen, who are themselves
created peers, and in practice it is a body very much of the
nature of the Canadian Senate whose members are appointed
for life. G. K. Chesterton's paradox that the great thing to
be said for the House of Lords is that it is so much more
democratic than the House of Commons cannot really be
sustained. It is very arguable that an assembly collected
by chance or lot or on the principles by which the voters of
a Gallup poll are collected would be more representative
of the ordinary man than an elected House of Commons
but it cannot be pretended that the House of Lords is such
as assembly. Nevertheless there is no doubt that the House
of Lords suffers in popular estimation through being
commonly referred to as an hereditary chamber, and it

would be better in the temper of modern times that peerages should become life peerages. This would have also the incidental advantage of remedying a small but most ridiculous injustice in our present constitutional arrangements— the injustice by which the eldest son of a peer is taken out of the House of Commons against his will on his parent's death and compelled to take his seat in the Lords.

It is true that the House of Lords must speak with the authority of tradition, or it speaks with no authority. No one would invent such a body and therefore, if it be reformed so drastically as to make it appear unrecognizable, its authority will be destroyed. Yet the creation of life peerages would not be a violation of tradition. It would be a return to tradition. No one except Mr. Herbert Morrison defends the House of Lords as it now is. Of old the Crown had such a power to create life peerages. The Stuart monarchs had considerable freedom whom they should summon to the House of Lords. This prerogative of the monarchy was one of the prerogatives destroyed by the Whig Revolution of 1688. The Tory tradition has never recognized an absolute hereditary right. In Lord Palmerston's Premiership Queen Victoria tried to revive this power to create life peers and was only prevented by the objection of the House of Lords itself that the power had been so long unused that it had lapsed. A quarter of a century before we find Canning, the Tory Prime Minister of the day, advocating that in exceptional circumstances the succession of a peerage should go to a second rather than to an elder son. "The remainder to Lord Norbury's second son", he writes to William IV, "appears to Mr. Canning at first sight a strong proposal; but, as the peerage must otherwise descend to the eldest son, who is an idiot, and as it appears to Mr. Canning (after some recent exhibitions in the House of Lords) peculiarly desirable to avoid among their lordships the number of specimens of irregular understanding. . . ."

Yet, if we are to imitate the Canadian example in making membership of the House of Lords a life appointment, we must be careful not to imitate it in making those appointments purely party appointments. If they are purely party appointments then the Upper House reflects a political complexion, which is not necessarily the complexion of the country to-day but which is the complexion which it had over the average of the past years. This is merely absurd. What is required for a revising chamber is a membership of distinguished and responsible statesmen, who sit loosely to party allegiance and who in no way accept a detailed party discipline, but, who, as far as they are of a party, are divided somewhere near equally between the parties. If the House of Commons is the House *table d'hôte*, it is all the more important that the Lords should be the House *à la carte*.

The present House of Lords has been at pains not to issue purely party challenges to the Socialist Government. It has attempted to revise bills in the sense of making them more workable and has been careful not to challenge the verdict of the Commons on the principle of the Bills. Fair-minded Socialists have often been ready to acknowledge that the Lords have done their work competently and conscientiously and that many Bills have been much improved by the Lords' Amendments. Nevertheless, so long as it is known that the Lords can at any time, if they wish to register a party vote, always register it in the Conservative sense, it would be unreasonable to expect the Socialist to be enthusiastic in his laudation of them. Nor is the argument sometimes adduced in certain Conservative circles that the Lords are to be preserved as a possible check on extravagant Socialist legislation at all a good one. So far from it being a Conservative interest that the Lords should have a large Conservative majority, it is obviously the Conservative interest that they should not have such a majority. Mr. Attlee may say that every Conservative scheme of reform is careful to preserve such a Conservative majority, but in fact every Conservative scheme of reform from that of Lord Salisbury, the great Prime Minister, to that of his grandson has always been particularly careful to provide a means for getting rid of that majority. The Lords have their veto, but they would entirely play into the hands of the Socialists were they

to use it. Nothing could possibly suit the Socialists better
than an election campaign in which their own more
controversial actions would be drowned beneath the cry
of "the Lords versus the People", if only they could be given
a colour of reason for that cry.[1]

It is possible, it is true, to imagine some Government
introducing legislation that was not only extremely foolish
but was also unpopular. A House of Commons, elected
on other issues, might see fit to defy the will of the people,
and then, it is sometimes argued, it would be right for the
Lords, like Bolingbroke's Patriot King, to appeal back to
the people against their elected representatives. But it is
very difficult indeed to think of circumstances under which
such action would be justified, unless, indeed, it be to throw
out an unjustified measure from the House of Commons
for the prolongation of its own life—a measure where the
Parliament Act rightly reserves to the Lords a full right of
rejection. But in general if the Government and the
Commons are really defying the will of the people, the best
way for the people to speak is through by-elections. No
Government, whatever its majority in Parliament, can
continue for long on a policy which is being condemned
by the electorate in by-election after by-election. Nor does

[1] The position to-day differs so widely from that of the years before the
Parliament Act that parallels are of little value. Yet there is a very general
misunderstanding of the acts of defiance of the Lords by the Commons in
those years. When the Lords threw out the Second Home Rule Bill, not
only had they reason to think—as the subsequent election proved—that the
electorate were on their side but even within the current Parliament the
majority of the British members of the House of Commons were on their side
and in opposition to the Bill. The Bill only passed the House of Commons
because of the votes of the Irish members. In the same way much ignorant
folly is talked about the defiance of the will of the people by the Lords when
they rejected the measures of the Liberal Government immediately before
the war of 1914. It is forgotten that at the elections of 1910 the Liberals and the
Conservatives were returned in almost equal strength and by a number of
by-election victories the Conservatives soon established themselves as the
strongest party. Those Liberal measures were only carried again by the
support of Irish votes. Mr. Redmond, whose own temperament on matters
of social reform was ultra-conservative, had made it quite clear that he had
no belief in these Liberal measures but that he supported them as a part
of the bargain for Liberal support of Home Rule. Whether these measures
were wise or unwise is as it may be, but the Lords had a very good case of
it that, in rejecting them, they were upholding the will of the people against
a conspiracy of the politicians in the Commons to frustrate it.

the argument make any better sense if we allow ourselves
to assume a revolutionary and tyrannical Government
which has suppressed by-elections and allows the people
no opportunity to express its opinions. Then we should have
a desperate situation in which there was no remedy save
in revolutionary action. But the House of Lords could clearly
provide no remedy, as it is not likely that a Government
which did not allow itself to be defeated at by-elections
would allow itself to be defeated in the House of Lords.
Therefore *cadit quæstio*.

But the question that remains is how the members of
the life House of Lords should be appointed. To leave them
all to the nomination of the Prime Minister and the Government, as in Canada, is to put too much power in the
Government's hands—far more power than at present when
the Prime Minister only makes a comparatively small number
of additions to a hereditary house. To appoint them by
some form of popular election would be, as Disraeli truly
saw, to make the House of Lords too much like the House of
Commons. To appoint them by the election on a restricted
property franchise would be too violently in contradiction
to the spirit of the age and would too greatly detract from
their prestige.

There is no reason why the holders of certain distinguished
posts—Bishops and representatives of all religious bodies,
Lord Mayors perhaps, Vice-Chancellors or representatives
of the universities, and so on—should not be *ex officio* members.
Yet, whatever elements of this sort it may be found desirable
to include in the new House of Lords, the main body of the
membership must certainly be nominated, and it is desirable
that nomination should not be by the Prime Minister alone
but by some small panel of members of the House of Commons, drawn in proportion to numbers in that House, or
some similar body, with an undertaking that the nominees
should be persons of distinction and that, so far as they had
party affiliations, the purpose should be to preserve an
approximate balance between the parties.

Yet even a reformed House of Lords could never be other

than a revising Chamber. As such, it is performing, and will continue to perform, a vital service. The more overloaded the time-table of the Commons becomes, the more the Commons are compelled to pass on to the Lords legislation that they either have not discussed at all or have not discussed adequately, the more important become the functions of the Lords. The House of Lords is clearly more important to-day than it has ever before been in English history. "With a perfect Lower House", wrote Bagehot, "it is certain that an Upper House would be scarcely of any value. If we had an ideal House of Commons perfectly representing the nation, always moderate, never passionate, abounding in men of leisure, never omitting the slow and steady forms necessary for good consideration, it is certain that we should not need a higher chamber. The work would be done so well that we should not want any one to look over or revise it." But to-day we have a House of Commons which is not only imperfect through the general imperfections of human nature, but which is compelled to work under conditions which make it impossible that its work be done well. Therefore we must indeed have a second Chamber. Yet a revising Chamber cannot of its very nature lighten the burden of work on the House of Commons. To the contrary, it adds to it; like a stern schoolmaster, compelling it to do again that which it has done ill.

But more important—at any rate for this purpose—than the reform of the Parliamentary system is the reform of the Cabinet system. At present the reality of decision on policy is slipping not only out of the hands of Parliament but also out of the hands of the Cabinet. Cabinet government is as much on its trial as Parliamentary government.

CHAPTER VII

THE REFORM OF THE CONSTITUTION

THE SOCIALISTS argue that restrictions on Parliamentary freedom are made necessary by the volume of legislation, that without such restrictions there would be no possibility of getting through the programme. To that argument it is very pertinently answered that there is no necessity to get through the programme at all. It is the Socialists themselves who have invented the necessity. At the outbreak of war, or at some other such time of crisis, then there is indeed a desperate necessity to rush through legislation in a hurry. The enemy, battering at the gates, will not allow Parliament to wait. But the Socialist Government, coming to office on the morrow of victory in war, had no need nor indeed excuse for hurry of this sort. Even if for the sake of argument we concede that it was desirable that the Bank of England, the mines, the transport system and all the rest should be nationalized, there was no conceivable reason why they should be nationalized in such a hurry. Indeed, if we are to credit the Socialist Government with any serious intention that their schemes should work, then there was every reason that they should not be nationalized in such a hurry. The condition of the success of Socialistic experiments is, as Sidney Webb showed, that they should be made slowly. Gradualness is not only desirable; it is inevitable. By the end of 1947 the country had run headlong into a gigantic economic crisis. But the legislative policy was not a defence against that crisis. It was far more true to say that the legislative policy was in part at least the cause of the crisis.

It is certainly true that the legislative policy was to a very large extent the cause of the crisis in the sense that it has taken our limited supplies of bureaucrats away from their proper business of administration and turned them to the preparation of these schemes of nationalization. As a result the administrative machinery has fallen into chaos. It has spread throughout the industrial world a general atmosphere of uncertainty about the future, which is the very last atmosphere in which schemes of reconstruction can be expected to breathe. On the economic plane, also, the lavish promises of the Socialists have caused a diversion of more labour than the nation could afford to capital schemes, whose best promise can only be increased wealth at some distant future date. "We have tried to do too much too quickly", sadly but truly confessed Mr. Attlee. Prating so largely about planning, the Socialists have jettisoned the traditional and only effective form of planning—planning through finance and through the Chancellor of the Exchequer. It is the traditional duty of the Chancellor to say to his colleagues, "There are these dozen things which you wish to do but we have only the resources to do three of them. We must select which three and we can then perhaps get these three done. Otherwise all that will happen will be that we start twelve things and finish none of them." This traditional planning duty was notoriously neglected under the Chancellorship of Dr. Dalton.

Yet for all that, whatever Government had been in power, whatever policy had been pursued, a large volume of legislation would have been necessary. That legislation might have had a less disruptive effect on the national life as a whole, but it is by no means certain, granted the existence of a tolerably powerful Opposition, that it would have made a smaller demand on Parliamentary time. The laws passed by another Government might have been less silly but there is little reason to think that they would have been less numerous. It took the Lloyd George Government after the 1914 war rather more laws to establish an anti-Socialist Commonwealth than it took the present Socialist Government after the recent war to establish a Socialist Commonwealth. Therefore it is only sensible to accept the proposition that, whatever Government may be in power, Parliament will have thrown upon it a burden of business, greater than it can properly perform whether in its volume

or in its nature, and that therefore, if freedom is to survive
at all and totalitarianism is to be avoided, some means must
be found of lightening the burden upon Parliament. This
is the major problem of the day, a problem to which the
Socialist party has no contribution to make whatsoever.

It is clear, as has already been stated, that we have not
got to-day, as the text-book so often tells us, Parliamentary
government.   We have got Cabinet government.   The
academic view is that Parliament is sovereign, that Parliament can enact any legislation that it chooses and that what
Parliament votes is the law.   But in reality Parliament
clearly cannot enact whatever legislation it chooses, because
Parliament can only vote on such legislation as the Government sees fit to submit to it. The trivial concession of a few
days of private members' time does not affect the substantial truth of this. This is no party point. The late Lord
Salisbury put it in 1929, when the Conservative Government
was in power, "Nothing", he said, "was more clear than
that, whatever party was concerned, the Government was
growing in importance every day. The Government was
absorbing more and more of the power which used to belong
to Parliament. Those who were familiar with public affairs
had seen the difficulty under which Parliament itself was
conducted, and how the power in the State was concentrated in the Government.   In regard to the House of
Commons, matters had undoubtedly been carried to such
a point that complete freedom of speech did not seem to be
any longer possible, and a good many details as to important
measures could never be discussed there."

What we have to-day is Cabinet government. Parliament, it is true, exists as a certain check on the omnipotence
of the Cabinet in the sense that Parliament can always bring
about the downfall of the Cabinet if sufficient of the supporters
of the Government turn against it to put it into a minority,
but the whole initiative of policy lies with the Cabinet,
nor would I advocate that it should be otherwise. The
initiative of policy must lie in a few hands, otherwise there
is intolerable instability and weakness of government,

as we found in the France of the Third Republic. Nevertheless, to admit that we ought to have Cabinet government
is not to admit that the present Cabinet system is incapable
of improvement. The test of experience has proved that it
is an idotic system. It grew up without reason or conscious
volition over the years before the 1914 war. Under the strain
of that war it collapsed.

The traditional system demanded that the heads of all
the important departments form the Cabinet, and Government policy be settled by Cabinet decision. No system could
be devised from which a coherent planned policy is less
likely to emerge, and, like the American Constitution,
the Cabinet system has only worked, so far as it has worked
at all, in periods when the great need was to prevent the
Government from doing things. Obviously all but the rarest
of Cabinet Ministers are predominantly interested in their
own departments and measure their success by their ability
in getting the Cabinet's attention for their departments.
A Cabinet of the traditional plan is little but a place of
competition between the different ministers to see who can
force his own schemes on to the agenda and decisions are
taken much more frequently for the purpose of preventing
rows and resignations than on any coherent principle. The
Cabinet Minister who brings informed criticism to bear on
the affairs of a department other than his own must be a
rarity and, where he exists, his activities are likely to be
resented rather than welcomed.

The great defect of the traditional Cabinet system was
that it was no one's business to do the Cabinet's general
thinking. The system was reduced to an absurdity under
Mr. Asquith's Coalition Government, which ruled from
May 1915 to November 1916. Never was there a time when
decisions and coherent policy were more needed. Yet the
political necessity to satisfy all wings and schools of thought
caused Mr. Asquith steadily to increase the size of the Cabinet,
until at last it reached the unwieldy number of twenty-two.
Mr. Asquith, having been Prime Minister before the war,
when the Liberal Government was under regular (and

incidentally particularly bitter) Parliamentary attack from the Conservative Opposition, was not well suited for the change to war and Coalition. Of him, as of Mr. Neville Chamberlain a quarter of a century later, it was felt that he was war-time Premier only through the accident that he happened to be there and not through any summons of the nation or through the possession of any pre-eminent gifts for war, and on this score Mr. Lloyd George who succeeded had an advantage of prestige over him, just as Mr. Churchill had an advantage of prestige over Mr. Chamberlain in our own time.

Mr. Lloyd George abolished the old Cabinet system, and substituted for it a new small Cabinet of statesmen, who could direct general policy in freedom from particular departmental responsibilities. The departmental heads had their pride assuaged by being told that they were of Cabinet rank but they no longer sat in the Cabinet. The Cabinet consisted of Mr. Lloyd George, Lord Milner, Lord Curzon, Mr. Bonar Law and Mr. Henderson. Of those, Mr. Bonar Law alone, leader of the Conservative party and Chancellor of the Exchequer, had a departmental responsibility.

That Cabinet won the war. The personalities in it changed but the system survived until the German defeat. After the German defeat Mr. Lloyd George continued with a Coalition Government but reverted to the traditional Cabinet system. It was a foolish and illogical compromise. If he wished to compromise, he would have been much better advised to have compromised in the opposite sense— to have returned to party government but to have preserved the reformed Cabinet system.

Ever since the Cabinet system, like the party system, has proved itself wholly unsuited for problems of the modern world and has collapsed whenever a strain has been placed upon it. Like the party system, it collapsed in 1931 and, like the party system, it collapsed again in 1940 and the country had to revert to small supra-departmental Cabinets. But politicians have a greater reluctance to break with the Cabinet system than they have to break with the party system. Under a coalition all the leading figures in all the parties—all those of sufficient standing to influence party decisions—have office and therefore they have no personal objection to it. But under the small, non-departmental Cabinet system statesmen of the very highest claims and distinction find themselves excluded from the Cabinet and from the inner sanctum of decisions. The reform of the Cabinet is therefore personally unpopular with politicians. Yet in spite of that the old traditional Cabinet system simply does not work under the pressure of modern circumstances. The only effect of the attempt to make it work is that the Prime Minister is compelled very largely to by-pass the Cabinet, to take decisions to an inordinate extent himself, and, it may be, to erect for himself some private secretariat or pseudo-Cabinet, wholly unknown alike to the constitution and to constitutional propriety.

The Prime Ministers who have held power since the end of the first World War have been statesmen of a wide variety of gifts. While all have had their abilities, few would claim that they have been of an ability outstandingly greater than that of any of their great predecessors. Yet they have been able to dominate Cabinets in a way in which none of the great figures of the nineteenth century could dominate them. This is true alike of Lloyd George, Baldwin, Chamberlain and Churchill, and a striking proof that the dominance arose not out of the personal quality of the Prime Minister but out of necessity and the nature of things is furnished by Mr. Keith Feiling's account of the *Life of Neville Chamberlain*. The contrast between Mr. Chamberlain's position as second man and his position as first man in the Government was extraordinary. At the time when he was Chancellor of the Exchequer and when he was doing most of the actual business of the Cabinet, he meekly accepted it that he could not have a major influence on a policy of which he disapproved. As soon as he became Prime Minister, he assumed for himself a predominance in the Cabinet perhaps more remarkable even than that of his predecessors. Bonar Law and Ramsay MacDonald, alone among inter-war

Prime Ministers, did not dominate their Cabinets, and of these Bonar Law was a sick man when he began his few months of Premiership and was hardly more than technically Prime Minister and Ramsay MacDonald was a miserable failure.

After the second World War, the Socialist party, which is always the party most strongly opposed to innovation on all matters other than those of direct Socialist dogma, reverted not only to the traditional and outworn form of Cabinet government but also to the eighteenth-century habit of having an unassuming, unimposing statesman as Prime Minister—Mr. Attlee—"the quiet little man with the quiet little voice", as Mr. Ernest Bevin ironically called him. But the experiment was a folly in anachronism.[1] It merely meant that for two years the country had no direction at all, and then Sir Stafford Cripps had to be appointed as a Mayor of the Palace to assume the reality of direction under the increasingly nominal leadership of the Merovingian puppet. Mr. Francis Williams in his *Triple Challenge* argues—and it is a matter on which he has every authority to argue—that the reality of control rests in an inner Cabinet of Mr. Attlee, Mr. Morrison, Mr. Bevin and Sir Stafford Cripps. But such an inner Cabinet, if it truly exists, lacks the essential nature of an inner Cabinet, which is that its members should be non-departmental. For one brief moment, while Sir Stafford Cripps had the direction of economic policy, freed from departmental responsibilities, it looked as if the Government had somehow blundered into progress. Then with Sir Stafford's appointment to the Exchequer it sunk listlessly back into its habitual reaction. The country may dislike being ruled by dynamic figures, and the experience of other countries may prove that it has great reason for its distaste. But the brutal truth is that the old-fashioned

---

[1] Mr. Winston Churchill in *The Gathering Storm* (p. 327) gives certain arguments against a non-departmental Cabinet as the director of a war. It is indeed true that, though this is an experiment that has usually been resorted to in war, it is in some ways better suited for peace than for war—because in war the final object of policy is given, to wit, to win the war. In peace it is far less certain, far more open to debate what we are in general aiming at. Who would venture to guess what Mr. Attlee is aiming at?

Cabinet system cannot work properly under any circumstances in the modern world, and it cannot work at all except under a Prime Minister who is prepared to assert himself ruthlessly against his colleagues. We must revert, not only in war-time and after the system has broken down, but at all times to a system, by which the thinking of the Government and its planning are done by a small Cabinet of men free from departmental duties and its execution is entrusted to the Departmental Ministers. There are a variety of plans, differing in detail—the Haldane Plan, Mr. Amery's plan, Lord Samuel's plan. Circumstance and personal accident will dictate which particular plan is adopted. But it is along that road alone that we can steer between the Scylla of planless chaos and administrative breakdown and the Charybdis of a dictatorial Prime Minister, governing not through the official Cabinet but through his private advisers, unknown to the constitution and irresponsible to the electorate.

Such a non-departmental Cabinet there must be. Yet what shall these thinkers think about? Their mere existence is no solution of our continuing difficulty that the organization of industry is a highly technical business and cannot be effectively controlled by non-technical politicians, whether they be Members of Parliament or Cabinet Ministers. It is no solution, as Mr. Harry Strauss so wittily said, just to throw another planner into the works.

The especial problem of freedom in our age is the problem of freedom in industry. In Victorian times it was not difficult to preserve political freedom because the matters upon which Liberals and Conservatives differed, the matters in which Government claimed to interfere, covered so small a part of human life. Gladstone and Disraeli could take their turns in power and breakfast, dinner, lunch and tea went on indifferent to their rise and fall. All that happened was that the Welsh Church was or was not disestablished, men voted by ballot or at the hustings, but the rest of life continued on its way undisturbed.

Whether our grandfathers should or should not have

demanded that their Governments tackle the problem of industry it is not necessary to inquire.   The fact is that they did not make this demand, and the fact is that our generation does make this demand.

To-day the Socialist from the one side of the fence and the old-fashioned capitalist from the other side may join to demonstrate that industry would produce much more efficiently if the people would agree not to interfere in its working.   Their demonstrations, however powerful in theory, are irrelevant.   We have moved into an age where men and women do not think themselves free unless they have some say in the industry in which they work.   If we are to preserve a free society, and even indeed if we wish to have satisfactory production, we must find a way in which to satisfy that demand.   We must find a real and not merely a metaphysical answer to that demand.   It is to no purpose to tell the ordinary man and woman that he has a share in the control of industry because industry is controlled by the state, which is his higher self, or by Parliament in the election of one member of which he had a fifty-thousandth part of a share.   To repeat the words of Mr. Peter Drucker, which I have made almost the text of this book, our problem is "to prevent centralized bureaucratic despotism by building a genuine local self-government in the industrial sphere".

How can we solve this problem?

Mr. Belloc's analysis in *The Servile State* remains substantially, indeed terrifyingly, true.   The potential slave-masters are indeed not, as he feared, the old capitalists but the much more dangerous new managers.   Yet it still remains that the only real solution lies in the wide distribution of property.   "If we do not restore the institution of property, we cannot escape restoring the institution of slavery.   There is no third course."   It is important, whenever possible, to preserve and strengthen the institutions of distributed property.   As far as possible everyone should be encouraged to own the house in which he lives and credit facilities should be provided to enable him to buy his own house as early as possible. People should be paid good wages and encouraged out of those wages to build up their own personal savings, which should be the normal source of relief for themselves and their families in the accidents of life. The State should only be the reliever of the exceptional calamity. Those who prefer the freedom, even if it be at the cost of a lower standard of living, of the life of a small holder, of a one-man business, of the intimate personal relationships of a small business, should certainly be allowed and encouraged to live such a life. Even in this age, age as it is of big business, over two hundred thousand of the two hundred and fifty thousand firms in this country employ less than ten workers. About half the total number of people employed in this country work in firms that employ less than 500 people.

We are told of the soul-destroying monotony of work in an office or in a large factory. The truth is that such work is utterly soul-destroying to some people, while there are others who would choose it for preference. As long as we have a variety of work, then each man and woman has at least an opportunity of finding work congenial to him. For this as well as for other reasons, it is important to preserve the small units in as great a strength as possible. For this reason, as well as for many other reasons, agriculture should be in every way encouraged—encouraged not only for its production of food but also for its production of men.

In agriculture there are the problems of prices and wages, of housing and amenities, of machinery and feeding-stuffs and the rest, with which we are all familiar. They are all important. But the greatest problem of all is how to remedy the defect in the structure of agriculture. It has been that great defect in the past that there has been insufficient opportunity for a man of energy and ability, born into an agricultural worker's family to better himself within agriculture. Consequently the able children in such families have tended to drift out of agriculture into industry and the towns. If labour is to be kept on the land, a way must be found of offering a career in agriculture to the man of ability. Small-holdings are useful for some people as a ladder by which they can rise from worker to farmer. It is one of the virtues of the new, mechanized farm that it provides many jobs, intermediate between that of farmer and worker, to which the worker of ambition can rise. While the Marxians talk to us of the growing rigidity of society's division into masters and men, the reality is in agriculture, as in industry, that modern developments are creating a society of an ever-increasing variety with un-numbered gradations between the top and the bottom, and this, among its many vices, is one of its great virtues. In agriculture, even more than in industry, it is important to recreate an integrated population—a population which belongs to the soil as much as the soil belongs to it. For the ultimate loyalty there must be owed to the land; the ultimate concern must be not with quick returns or with immediate production but to hand on the land in as good a condition of fertility as it was received. The great problem of the age—in every country—is the problem of the con-servation of the soil. This problem cannot be solved by rootless men or those who live only for the day.

Yet, foolish as are rigid generalizations in view of the enormous variety of the modern world, in general the drift of the times is towards larger units—indeed by a paradox, the small units are to a large extent only able to survive because the essential services of the nation are performed by large units which can perform them with a cheapness and efficiency that only combination has made possible. New power developments in electricity or atomic energy may in the future increase the economic efficiency of the small unit—or they may not. It may be that in quite a few years' time developments of atomic power will have made a coal-mine as great an anachronism as a rushlight candle, and the unit of production be once more the small unit. Who can say? These things will be as they will be. The present drift is the other way. It is drifting that way, not as the incor-rigible moralist will tell us, because of the wickedness of the masters of combines and cartels, but because this is the inevitable drift demanded by the needs of efficiency. The Socialist, as I have argued, is mistaken in saying that there is a drift towards monopoly but he is right in saying that there is a drift towards big units. It is futile to attempt to check this drift by Anti-Trust Laws. Laws cannot compel two people to stay apart, when they both want to combine. Anti-Trust Laws have not been very effective in America; they are likely to be far less effective here. Mass production is by far the most efficient method of production in many industries. In America with her gigantic market an industry can be divided among a number of firms and each of them be large enough to employ methods of mass production. This is what happens in the American steel industry. In this country with its smaller market combines may be necessary in order to make the unit of production large enough for efficiency. We must accept the fact of the big unit where it is needed and see how we can solve our problem of freedom within it.

The pretence that that problem can be solved by a yearly debate on the workings of a nationalized industry in a Parliament of inexpert politicians is an absurdity. The managers' powers can only be efficiently controlled if they are submitted to the criticism of those who work within the industry, whose profession therefore compels them to know what they are talking about and who will attack the problems on their intrinsic merits and not through party formulae. We must have measures of self-government of industry.

Chapter VIII

RESPONSIBILITY IN INDUSTRY

WE CANNOT solve this, any more than any other problem, unless we first state it fairly and realistically. Much debate about the capitalist system in the past has been rendered idiotic by the erection of the capitalist into an absurd bogy-man, incapable of virtue. It would be no less disastrous an idiocy to make such a bogy-man of the new manager. It would be as foolish to ascribe to him an immaculate conception and to imagine that he, alone of men, will be found impervious to all the corrupting temptations of power.

We can then only hope to solve the problem if we begin by understanding that there is a genuine dilemma. Efficient management is necessary for industry. Management has its rights, and we cannot hope that our industrial problems will be solved, unless those rights are fully conceded. We can easily throw things into chaos if out of ideological sentimentality we submit managers to direct election or submit them to such popular control as makes it impossible for them efficiently to do their duty. Again in this, as in other problems, there is grave danger of oversimplification. The old cartoons used to represent the capitalist as one bloated gentleman with a top-hat and a large cigar. The reality was that shares were owned by a very wide variety of people of very different incomes and social circumstances. So, too, manager is a vague word. A manager is in strict definition anyone who has any sort of responsibility for the work of anybody other than himself, and in this sense everyone from the General Manager down to the foreman is to a greater or less extent a manager. It might well be argued that of all forms of consultation one of the most important and the least developed is that between manage-

ment and management, between the higher management and
the lower management.

However that may be, we cannot hope to find a solution
unless we see the problem not as one of a conflict between
good and evil, a wrestling of Ormuzd against Ahriman
but as a problem of reconciling two genuine necessities—
the necessity to give adequate authority to the manager
and the equal necessity to give adequate responsibility to
the worker. Nor indeed is the problem fairly, indeed sanely,
stated if it is stated as a conflict of the worker against the
manager. On the contrary, all but the smallest-minded and
most foolish among managers are the first themselves to insist
that the most important of all their tasks is that of creating
among their workers a full sense of partnership in their work.

Since the very beginnings of industrialism there have
always been men who have wrestled with this problem of
reintegration to which we have referred, the problem of
giving to the factory worker some share of responsibility
for the work which he has to do. The problem was first
notably tackled by Robert Owen, who tried to solve it
along the lines of complete self-government in industry
for the workers. In 1833 under his inspiration there was
created the Grand National Guild of Builders, which aspired
to capture the whole building industry. According to its
constitution the qualification for a master-builder was to
be direct election by his fellow workmen. But, attacked from
without and rent by faction within, the Guild collapsed.

A similar fate overtook a number of other experiments in
Producers' Co-operatives, which were made in the 1870's
—the Ouseburn Engine Works started by a group of
Newcastle engineers, a Co-operative Mining Company of
some Northumberland and Durham miners, Shireland
colliery in South Yorkshire, the Leicester Hosiery Operatives'
and so on. In general the experiments have not proved
successful. Self-governing workshops, said the Webbs in
What Syndicalism Means, "fail to command either the amount
of capital required, or the managerial ability, or the necessary
knowledge of the market, or the workshop discipline, with-

out all of which efficient production is impossible." On the other hand, the printing industry has provided a notable exception to this general record of failure, and a number of Producers' Co-operatives have flourished and still continue to flourish in that industry.

The doctrine of the works for the workers, rather than the works for either the capitalist or for the State, received its philosophic formulation on the Continent under the name of Syndicalism, *syndicat* being the French word for trade union, and was put forward by the Industrial Workers of the World in the United States. But both the continental syndicalists and the Industrial Workers of the World were apostles of violence, who rejected political action and demanded unceasing strikes until the capitalist machine was brought to a standstill. Their tactics could have brought nothing but ruin to the workers of this country and never won any serious following here.

An attempt was, however, made in the movement of Guild Socialism under the leadership of Mr. G. D. H. Cole and Mr. R. H. Tawney, immediately before and after the 1914 war, to weld some of the ideas of Syndicalism into the ideas of Socialism. According to the Guild Socialist theory, industries were to be owned by the State but conducted by the workers—by the National Guild. The word "guild", a conscious mediaevalism, was preferred to Syndicate, because it was desired that all who worked in the industry, irrespective of grade, should have a voice in management and that the control of management should not be confined to the members of the Trade Union.

According to Mr. Cole's *Self-Government in Industry* in each shop there would be shop Committees elected by the ballot of all the workers in the shop. There would also be a Works Committee for works as a whole, District Committees, a National Guild Executive and a National Delegate meeting, all similarly elected by direct ballot. Foremen and Works Managers would be elected by ballot and the General Managers and Works' experts selected by the Works' Committee.

An experiment in Guild Socialism was tried out in the building industry after the 1914 war, but it was not successful. Of existing Trade Unions the Post Office Workers still carry on active propaganda for Guild Socialism and proclaim among their objects "the organization of Post Office workers into a comprehensive industrial union, with a view to the service being ultimately conducted and managed by a Guild."

The records of the past are sufficient to show that experiments of self-government in industry are more easily advocated and undertaken than carried through to success, and, if a task is difficult, we serve no man if we deny its difficulty. But it is yet more absurd to say that something is impossible just because it is difficult. The fact is that, though the solution may not be easier to come by to-day than it was a hundred years ago, there is a much greater urgency to find a solution now than there was then. The situation is more urgent now than it was then for two reasons. First, in the early days of industrialism, industrialism was less widespread than it is to-day and it was easier for the man who could not tolerate its monotony and its irresponsibility to find alternative occupation—whether on the land in this country or through emigration overseas. Secondly—and more important—we have to face the inevitable consequences of education.

Those consequences are not wholly good, but, even where they are bad, it is useless to shut our eyes to them. Education has destroyed much culture. It has produced a generation which cannot live without unending doses of dehumanizing mechanical amusements—

> "decent, godless people,
> Their only monument the asphalt road
> And a thousand lost golf-balls",

as Mr. T. S. Eliot wrote in *The Waste Land*. That is evil and degrading. The great culture of Christendom has a higher destiny than to provide people with a few more cinemas and a few more cigarettes. But it has also produced a generation which demands a larger share of responsibility in its work than was necessary for its grandparents. The cultural gap between master and man is far narrower to-day than it was a hundred years ago, and that narrowing of the gap must be recognized in industrial arrangements. This is a good consequence of education—a consequence not the less good if some of the problems which it sets are difficult and the solution of them not immediately obvious. There is an intolerable strain and paradox about a system which teaches the ordinary man in the street that he is a fit judge whether Burma should be granted her independence or the Welsh Church should be disestablished but is not a fit judge where he himself should work for his living or what wages he should receive. The problem, if it is not to be solved under slavery, can only be solved under industrial democracy. There is no third course. The machine has perhaps on balance saved the worker from more drudgery than it has imposed on him. Much uncreative work that used to be done by hand is now done by power. But there is this great difference between the old drudgery and the new. In nineteenth-century industrialism the greater the intelligence and initiative of the worker, the more valuable he was as a worker. But the technological revolutions of the twentieth century have created a profoundly new and disturbing problem. To-day over wide fields of industry, the less intelligence and the less initiative the worker has, the more valuable he is as a worker. In the most completely mechanical of the "conveyor belt" jobs intelligence and initiative are a positive disadvantage. The high intelligence is less likely to be able to stand the monotony of them than the low intelligence.

It is no longer a question whether we solve this problem or whether we ignore it. We cannot ignore it or treat it as a sentimental frill, to be postponed and considered in less urgent times. We hear much of the menace of Communism, and it may indeed be necessary to take certain immediate offensive measures to repel Communism. But we cannot defeat Communism merely by being against it.

Now, as I have argued, the great problem of the day is to give to the ordinary man and woman a sense of responsibility and purpose for which to live. Both Nazism and Communism have singularly failed to solve that problem within the round of the daily life of business and industry and have therefore been compelled—it was a compulsion, not a choice, for their leaders—to find a false solution by drugging the minds of their subjects with the vision of fantastic threats and menaces from outside. They have been forced back on to the traditional tyrants' remedy of "busying giddy minds with foreign quarrels"—with results that are in the end disastrous alike for the tyrants, for their subjects and for all mankind. The great modern problem is to find a way of keeping people sane without making them apathetic.

Let us then have the freest discussion how we shall integrate the worker into the industrial machine, but let us understand that, though there is every room for difference of opinion about any particular solution, yet the problem has to be solved and a way has to be found if our civilization is to survive. Whatever our politics may be, we shall be guilty of a fatal mistake if we relapse into complacency because, it may be, at the moment we are in possession of an electoral majority. As Mr. Churchill truly and characteristically said in his Romanes lecture, "Economic problems, unlike political issues, cannot be solved by any expression, however vehement, of the national will, but only by taking the right action. You cannot cure cancer by a majority. What is wanted is a remedy."

Out of the Guild Socialist propaganda there emerged during the 1914 war the Shop Stewards' Movement. Wise statesmanship saw that it would be both dangerous and illogical if the workers' legitimate demand for a share in responsibility should take a form sheerly hostile to the existing organization of industry. On the contrary, if the problem was seen in proportion, then the prosperity of industry was an interest both to the nation at large and to all engaged in industry in whatever capacity and the true task of statesmanship was to talk as little as possible about "the two sides of industry", to emphasize as little as possible the matters upon which interests were divided and as much as possible the matters upon which their interests were in common. In 1916 the Whitley Committee was established in order to discover ways in which "the workpeople should have a greater opportunity of participating in the discussion about and the adjustment of those parts of industry by which they are most affected". Out of this emerged the National Joint Industrial Councils of which many were established in the years immediately after the 1914 war. A similar spirit inspired the Mond-Turner conversations at the same time—conversations which received the blessing alike of the Employers' Confederation, of the Federation of British Industries and of the Trade Union Congress but which for some reason that is even yet not quite clear were never brought to a practical conclusion.

The Guild Socialists criticized the Joint Industrial Councils on the ground that what they wanted was "workers' councils" and that they were being fobbed off instead with "consultation". The outbreak of the Russian Revolution filled Western Socialists with high ambitions of a direct and complete workers' control of industry. But, as we know, that phase of Soviet experiment was very shortlived and it was not long before the manager was brought back to the Russian factory and established in power a great deal more dictatorial than he had ever enjoyed under the old régime. The collapse of the Russian and of similar Italian experiments led Socialists in Britain and elsewhere to be much more cautious in defining the field within which direct election was practicable than they had previously been. Guild Socialism declined, and Socialist thinking turned to the Public Board as the organ for government of nationalized industry. It gave itself to the debate whether there should be direct Trade Union representation on these Public Boards.

In 1915 the Trade Union Council had demanded "increasing democratic control in nationalized industries". In 1917 the railwaymen had made a demand for such control and in 1918 the miners. In 1920 a building Guild was established. But the years, 1929-1931, the years of the second Labour Government saw the clash between Mr. Herbert Morrison and the Transport and General Workers' Union under Mr. Bevin on this point. In 1932 an attempt was made to commit the Trade Union Council to governing boards, to which appointments were to be made solely on the ground of fitness. This was referred back for further consideration. By 1936 the Transport and General Workers' Union was pacified but Mr. Dukes and the General and Municipal Workers took up the cry for direct representation. But in 1944 the Trade Union Congress in its Interim Report on Post-War Reconstruction reached the definite conclusion that any trade unionist appointed to a Public Board "should surrender any position held in, or any formal responsibility to the Trade Union". The reasons for this decision were two. On the one hand, it was recognized that it would be improper that any member of such a managerial board should have a divided loyalty, even as it would be improper were a Cabinet Minister to have such a divided loyalty. On the other hand, it was thought that if the Trade Union had its official representative on the managerial board, then its hands would no longer be free to criticize managerial policy.

In any event that was the decision reached by the Trade Union Congress in 1944, and of course, as we know, the policy of the Socialist Government has been in accordance with that decision. But, what is important to note is that in spite of the reluctance of Trade Union leaders to accept any positive responsibility for policy—a reluctance that was entirely intelligible in view of their traditional role as an essentially critical body—circumstances compelled them to accept a great deal of such positive responsibility during the war. They, together with the employers, were represented on the Ministry of Labour's National Joint Advisory Council and locally on the Regional Boards and District Production Committees, Yard Committees and Site Committees. These tasks were tasks, patriotically undertaken, but tasks, as those who understood them well knew, which were in breach of the traditional function of the Trade Union, which is of its essence a critical body, responsible for bargaining for wages and conditions of labour against the employer, whether that employer be State or private individual. The Trade Union leaders were well aware that they were weakening their personal positions and giving hostages to jealous rivals by accepting even such limited constructive responsibility during the war. They did it with their eyes open and from patriotic motives. Even after the war they have continued to send their representatives to such bodies as the National Production Advisory Council, the Development Council, the Ministry of Supply's Advisory Councils and so on. But the Trade Unions rightly refuse to allow themselves to be officially associated with responsibility for the management of industry, nor on the other hand do we solve the problem of giving the worker responsibility in his work merely by saying that his Trade Union has been consulted. The curse of the modern world of gigantic units is its metaphysical frauds. What men and women want is the right to speak through their own mouths, not to have their supposed needs and those of sixty thousand of their fellow citizens voiced for them by an elected or appointed representative, whether he be a Member of Parliament or Trade Union delegate. It is indeed a valid criticism of the old capitalism that, when it spoke of freedom, it meant too often only freedom for the capitalist, and, when it said "Set the people free", it meant "Set the capitalist free". It failed to provide a place of responsibility for the worker. But that evil is clearly in no way remedied by transferring power from the capitalist to the State or the manager. The worker still remains as irresponsible as ever.

Such Socialist literature as adverts to the problem at all is curiously apt to think that it has solved the problem of giving representation to the worker if only it has succeeded in giving representation to the Trade Union. But this is the very opposite of a solution. As has already been said, men join Trade Unions just as men take shares in companies

not because they want a share in responsibility but because
they want somebody else to take responsibility for them. It
is the common complaint of the Trade Unionist, in his
controversy with the Communists, that the ordinary Trade
Union member will not be bothered to turn up to meetings.
The statistics seem to show that four out of five Trade Unionists never attend a branch meeting. We cannot claim that the
problem of workers' representation is solved so long as we
only hear the voice of the Trade Union leader. We can only
claim that it is solved when we hear the voice of the worker
himself.

The old-fashioned critic is inclined to grumble that endless
consultations with the workers are a waste of time, a luxury
and a drag on efficiency, that what is needed is to get on
with the job. The evidence is all the other way. Professor
Elton Mayo, for instance, in his *Social Problem of an Industrial
Civilization* tells the story of the Hawthorne Works of the
Western Electric Company. As a result of consultation with
the workers, various changes and improvements were
introduced there in order to test their effect on output.
Output rose. Then—again after consultation with the
workers and simply to test the effect—the improvements
were all withdrawn. But still output continued to rise, and
the cause of its rise, it was discovered, was not the encouragement of any of the improvements as such but the encouragement that the workers derived from the fact of being
consulted.

Mr. Peter Drucker in his *Big Business* tells another story
of an aircraft factory on the west coast of America, where no
concession of wages or conditions had any success in improv-
ing the bad morale of the workers. Eventually it was discovered that the workers had never seen any of the planes
that they were making and did not know the purpose of the
part which they had to produce. A bomber was brought
down and placed in the factory grounds. The workers were
invited to come with their wives and children and sit in it.
They were shown the particular part on which they were
working, and its importance was explained to them. The

result was an instant and enormous improvement in morale.

Old-fashioned reactionaries like Mr. Zilliacus often speak of the American as an extreme Right-wing régime, and others speak of the desirability of choosing some third middle way between the extremes of American capitalism and Russian Communism. Such language, like most language which speaks of the conflict between capitalism and Socialism as a reality, has little meaning. American capitalism has gone far further than either British or Russian Socialism in the direction of true industrial democracy. In America, a recent article in a technical journal tells us, forty-seven out of every hundred firms issue advance information about changes in price and design to their employees before they issue them to their customers. Fifty-five out of a hundred fully explain promotion prospects to their employees. One in four give detailed explanations of profits and their relations to wages. One in ten issue their financial reports to workers as well as shareholders. Fifty-two out of a hundred send regular personal letters of the firm's financial position to all their employees. There is incomparably more consultation between labour and capital under American capitalism than under any socialistic system.

Therefore it is of the first importance that the Joint Production Council and the Works Council in this country should be preserved and strengthened in every way possible. The principle must be so extended that every worker who wishes to do so can find some place where he has a right to go and to make such suggestions as he sees fit, and, of course, where a suggestion is not adopted, the worker must be given a full and proper statement why it is not adopted. Such machinery must be kept quite distinct from the conciliation machinery, which of its very nature exists to reconcile rival interests. If production is to be maintained, then discipline and the proper rights of management must be safeguarded. All experience goes to prove that the direct election of managers is not practicable. But in all matters that are not directly connected with production—in the

firm's recreation and sport—there should be absolute
equality between man and master. There are matters on
which there is an inevitable rivalry of interests, but there are
also matters upon which there is a common interest. It is
the common interest of all engaged in an industry in whatever capacity that production should be as abundant and
efficient as possible. It may perhaps be for the moment
inevitable that members of joint production committees
or of works' councils should sit there as representatives of
"the two sides" of industry but the more that they can
discuss these problems upon which the interests of the
"two sides" are identical, the more that they can discuss
those problems on their intrinsic merits and not from the
point of view of their particular "side" the better. If in the
future a day should come when it is possible to elect members
to these committees and councils simply for their own
personal qualities and in indifference to the "side" from
which they come, that would be indeed a day of progress.
After all, if industry cannot agree within itself what it wants,
then there is no alternative to unconditional surrender to the
managerial revolution.

It is clear that this need of integration exists alike in
nationalized and in unnationalized industries. Nationalization is no solution nor is the absence of nationalization a
solution. Within the nationalized industries we certainly
have a right to insist on the establishment of full consultative
machinery and of a road for the two-way passage of ideas
from top to bottom and from bottom to top. It is a debatable
question to what extent legislative compulsion should be
used in private industry. Obviously the less compulsion and
dictation the better. It is obviously far better that the
individual firm should establish its own works council and
that firms should have freedom to vary its form in detail in
order to meet their own particular circumstances. If any
compulsion has to be brought to bear on the recalcitrant
and the reactionary, it is much better that compulsion be
imposed by the industry rather than by the Government.
We are often told that the issue is between control or no

control. Like so many of the much trumpeted dilemmas of to-day, it is a false dilemma. Certain controls there must be, but in this matter, as in others, those controls should be to a much greater extent imposed by industry on itself and to a much less extent imposed by the Government upon industry.

The Socialist Government are perfectly right in thinking almost no price too high in order to prevent the reappearance of unemployment, for unemployment has become to the workers the very symbol of frustration. Yet it is far from certain that the Socialists, like the traditional Blimps of the War Office, are not fighting the next war with the weapons of the last and the next depression with the weapons of the last. Compulsory insurance is no remedy against unemployment. It is a mere trick of words. The unemployment fund is patently too large for casual needs and too small to meet a major depression. But supposing that industry itself gives a guaranteed long-term contract to, say, two-thirds of its workers—the married or those who have been with it five years? The worst depression would not be so severe that a major firm could not fulfil such a contract, while it would be no great hardship to the young and the unmarried that they should provide that element of fluidity in our labour which a developing and flexible society needs. The state need then only step in as the remedy against exceptional calamity. Nor should we forget that the most effective form of compulsion still remains to-day what it has always been in the past—that the inefficient and old-fashioned firm is compelled, even perhaps against its wish, to take up efficient and modern methods or else to be driven out of business by its more up-to-date competitors.

Sir Stafford Cripps said on September 12th, 1947, that, if there was inordinate delay in the establishment of Production Committees "we shall be obliged to take steps to enforce their constitution". It is very much to be hoped that this threat will never be carried out. No one in the early days of the experiment could fairly demand of the Government a pledge that it would at no point use one iota of compulsion, but the main function of a wise Government will certainly be one of advice, encouragement, education, the provision of training as through the Training Within Industry system of the Ministry of Labour and the like. The attempt of a Government to impose upon the doctors a health scheme to which the vast majority of the doctors are bitterly opposed would be in any event foolish, whether the doctors' objections were well founded or ill founded.

It is coming increasingly to be understood that medicine and psychiatry have a much larger contribution to make in industry than was guessed at by our ancestors. Health is important, both for immediate production and for the solution of the deeper problem of creating an industrial society of which every worker can feel himself truly to be a member. It has been calculated that ill health is responsible for the loss of two hundred and seventy times as many man-hours as strikes or lock-outs, and the volume of it can certainly be reduced. I do not pretend to any sort of competence to enter into any controversies that there may be about details of either medical or psychiatric treatment. The Industrial Health Research Board, set up in the 1914 war, the National Institute of Industrial Psychology, the Tavistock Institute of Human Relations, the Industrial Welfare Society, the new training unit at Roffey Park Rehabilitation Centre, Sir George Schuster's work on the Committee of Industrial Productivity—all these and many others have their important contribution to make. The basic principle of psychiatry is a principle exactly suited to industrial relations. Unlike the old-fashioned schoolmaster or the old-fashioned doctor, the psychiatrist does not impose a cure. He diagnoses. Where something is wrong, he tell people what is really wrong—which is very often something quite different from what they imagine to be wrong— and then encourages them to impose the remedy on themselves.

Chapter IX

INDUSTRIAL PARLIAMENT

SELF-GOVERNMENT in industry might mean any of three things. It might mean a general Parliament of Industry as advocated in the plan for a National Industrial Council, in the debate on the Address in February, 1919, in the Webbs' *Constitution of a Social Commonwealth for Great Britian* and in Mr. Churchill's Romanes Lecture of 1930. It might mean measures of self-government in each industry on the lines of the Whitley Councils or of Mr. G. D. H. Cole and Professor Tawney's Guild Socialism. It might mean Works Councils or Joint Industrial Councils within the particular firm or factory.

There is a need for organizations at all these three levels. Obviously, in so far as the main object of all these schemes is to create in the worker a feeling that he is now associated as a partner in his industry, it is essential to have factory— and firm—organizations. For the main point of these schemes is that they should be schemes with which the ordinary worker can be associated, and the ordinary worker cannot spend his days in attending national meetings. The greatest danger in industry is unnecessary centralization and it is of the first importance that all matters that can be settled locally should be so settled. In the small business the worker can often be most easily taken into confidence and consultation without a formal organization. In large businesses a more formal works-organization is necessary, and at this level—as a general rule, at any rate—the decision can be taken what schemes of co-partnership, share-distribution to employees or profit-sharing are suitable to the particular business, what possibilities there are of giving the workers increased security by giving them longer terms of contract—say, yearly contracts—and so on. Even within a single industry one scheme suits one firm and another suits another. But at the same time there are certain rules of the game—conditions of labour and wages in each industry —which it is desirable to settle nationally. For these organizations of the nature of Whitley Councils are desirable. The greater number of the problems of an industry it is best to leave to those concerned in that industry to settle.

Yet it would be dangerous to have no organization of industrial self-government above those of the particular industry. The depression of the years between the wars was mainly due to a faulty financial policy. But there were also purely industrial causes for it. In the nineteenth century the whole world had been dependent on the basic British industries—coal, ship-building, iron and steel and textiles. Because these were the oldest industries and the first to be put on a basis of modern power-driven production, they were the first industries that other countries developed, when they came to industrialize themselves. As a result supply in them became redundant, and in the years between the wars these industries were in a depressed condition not only in Britain but in every country in the world. They only appeared to be in a more depressed condition in Britain because a larger proportion of labour was employed in them here than in other countries. On the other hand the years between the wars were by no means years of universal depression in this country. The new industries—the electrical, engineering and motor industries—flourished exceedingly. The total national income increased enormously.

It is therefore clear that what we needed during those years was fluidity of labour. We suffered because labour— for many reasons, some of them unavoidable—was imperfectly fluid. And what was true of those years will certainly be true of the years ahead. The precise pattern no man can foresee. But it is certain that some industries will go up and others will go down, that a redistribution of labour will be necessary, that the nation whose labour is rigidly distributed will be at a great disadvantage and that the nation whose labour can easily and without social dislocation move from industry to industry will be at a great advantage. Above all, it is certain in our particular case that we shall need more men in agriculture.

That being so, we shall greatly handicap ourselves if we so organize our industry that each person belongs definitely to one industry and to no other and can only with the greatest difficulty move from job to job. If there is no machinery of industrial self-government above that of the particular industry, then there will be an inevitable danger that redundant industries will fight to compel the nation to take artificial measures to maintain employment of full numbers within a particular industry instead of recognizing, as may well be the case, that what the national interest really requires is a reduction of labour in that particular industry and its redistribution to other industries.

Again, the common talk about monopoly's destruction of competition ignores the fact that, the less competition there is within an industry, the more competition there is between industries. There are many different sorts of competition. There is not merely the simple straightforward competition for a market between two manufacturers of the same article. There is also the competition between articles for the favour of the public. Shall the public spend its money on reading or motoring? Tea or coffee? Booze or baseball? Guns or butter? There is the competition between different industries for labour.

> "How you're going to keep 'em
> Down on the farm
> After they've seen Paree?"

How are we to attract labour into the mines? There is the competition between manufacturers of different products for the same raw materials. All want coal. Most want steel. The supplies are limited. Who shall get them? There is the competition between rival manufacturers for which shall have the right to import different raw materials. These matters, say the defenders of the old political economy, will all be settled by the price-mechanism, if only we allow it to operate freely. There is much coherence in the argument. But will it be possible, whatever may be theoretically desirable, to allow the price-mechanism to operate freely? Will we have time to allow its processes to work themselves out? If you interfere with the mechanism at one place, it is easy to upset the whole delicate equilibrium. Unforeseen consequences follow and you are compelled to other interferences that had never been intended.

Under what may be called the capitalist-trade union economy wages were settled by "collective bargaining"— by an agreement between the employers and the Trade Union, representing the workers. Labour was distributed —or at least was supposed to be distributed—by incentives. That is to say, labour was supposed to be attracted into industries in which it was especially wanted by the offer of higher incentives—which meant, principally, by higher wages.

The Trade Unions to-day, resolute in their opposition to what is called a "wages policy", are determined to preserve this system of separate negotiations in separate industries. No one who is nervous at the aggressions of the state can fail to sympathize with their determination. Yet we must understand the difficulties of their conservative policy. Wages are to be settled by collective bargaining and it is important that they be settled in such a way as to effect a proper distribution of labour. But it is clear that the method will only effect the purpose if those unions to whom the public interest most requires the attraction of labour have also the strongest bargaining power. But is this so? Unfortunately it is by no means so. On the contrary, there are two sorts of industries—those which can easily pass an increase of costs on to the consumer and those who cannot get at their consumers. The industry which performs some essential service for the public at home—for instance, a railway—is an example of the first sort. If the railways grant an increase of wages and by consequence increase their costs, they can obtain permission to increase their

fares and rates and the public has no alternative but to pay
the increased fares, or alternatively, under nationalization,
they can increase their losses and send in the bill to the taxpayer. An industry working for export—for instance, coal—
is an example of the second sort. At the moment we are
living in the last days of a sellers' market, but, when there
is not a sellers' market, then it is not possible for the National
Coal Board to increase the cost of exported coal, because,
if it does so, the foreigner refuses to buy. Therefore, the
unsheltered industry, which has to keep down costs or die,
finds it difficult with all the will in the world to raise wages.
Indeed, worse than that, it may even find it difficult to
maintain wages. For the unsheltered industry is itself the
consumer of the sheltered industry. It uses transport; it
uses raw material, and, supposing that labour in the
sheltered industries has demanded wage increases and the
employers have quite readily granted those wage increases,
confident that they can pass them on to the consumer, then
the Coal Board finds itself in a position of being unable to
market its goods at a higher price, when it is at the same time
having to meet higher costs of production. Far from being
able to increase wages it may find it very difficult not to
reduce them. Yet these export industries are the key
industries to which it is particularly important to attract
labour. An unco-ordinated Trade Union policy, so far from
offering the incentives where they are socially desirable,
makes it mathematically impossible to offer those incentives.
That is why the Government has been forced back on the
odious alternative of trying to distribute labour by direction.

Is there a half-way house between direction and free
bargaining? Can we find a half-way house in some "wages
policy" by which the Government settles what wages are
to be in the various industries and then allows those wages
to have their full effect in distributing labour in the way
that is socially desirable? Obviously a Government could—
in theory, at any rate—fix all wages and keep all wages down
in the sheltered industries and perhaps make a particular
exception for some particular industry, producing for the

home market, into which it desired to attract labour. But no Government, however totalitarian, could raise the wages of an under-manned industry, working for the export market, in order to attract labour into that industry. Or at least the only way in which it could do so would be by subsidizing the product on the export market. To that there are two objections. First, we have agreed not to do this by the Washington Agreement and such action would bring against us accusations of dumping from other nations and retaliatory action. Second, the subsidy must come out of the pockets of the rest of the community—from the sheltered industries, which are by definition in an exceptionally favourable position for resisting attacks upon themselves.

The issue is not any longer between capital and labour. The issue is between one industry and another—to persuade an industry in a favourable position not unduly to press its advantages and to give a fair deal to the industry in an unfavourable position. As long as the sham offensive against capitalists was maintained, it was hopeless to expect the workers to see the issue in real terms. A failure of wages in an unsheltered industry was complacently blamed on the wicked capitalists, and the workers in the sheltered industries never dreamed for an instant of their share in the responsibility for their comrades' misfortune. Now that we have passed beyond the age of that sterile and foolish debate between labour and capital, there is a greater chance that the workers in every industry will understand the total problem of industry and accept with moderation the particular place which the needs of society mark out for them. But they cannot do so unless industry and industry meet face to face and have a formal and public opportunity of laying their difficulties before one another.

How then can this problem be solved?

I do not think that it can be solved by debates in the political Parliament or by party politicians. The party system is too far gone in decay for that. The public—rightly or wrongly—no longer believes the party politicians sufficiently to take the truth from them. This may be unfortunate and it may to some extent be unfair, but it is, I fear, true. The public thinks of party politicians as entertainers putting on an act, as barristers talking to a brief, compelled by their profession to say that all that the other side says is wrong and all that their own side says is right. It is coming to believe that the real decisions are taken elsewhere than in Parliament and are little influenced by electoral results or by the accident which party is in power. Elections merely decide what the policies shall be called, not what they really are, and the party game is, in the eyes of a large proportion of the electorate, a boring and expensive circus to which they are cajoled to contribute but whose real purpose is rather to divert the attention of the public from what is going on than to give the public a method of controlling it.

No one has better means of knowing than the present writer that there are many politicians in all parties of whom this is monstrously unfair. Indeed the politician is often justified in throwing back the blame on to the public. It is often the politician who tries to discuss these questions with sanity, and the public which insists upon obscuring them beneath the insane farrago of clichés and catchwords with which all questions that can be compressed into party issues are in these days bespattered. But we are suffering from the sins of a long line of party bosses, stretching from Disraeli to Mr. Herbert Morrison, who have taken the very reasonable device of a loose organization of party and tightened it into an absurdity. A question that becomes a party question is incapable of solution simply because it is never properly described, and this question can only be solved if it is taken and kept out of party politics.

There are only three lines of solution. The one is to go boldly forward to the full, totalitarian, stark solution to which a sort of bastard logic appears to lead—to impose solutions of all these problems, whether those solutions be accepted or not, and to shrink from no weapon in the imposition of them. That would be horrible, and I do not believe that in the last resort it would work in such a country as ours. Or again, it might in theory be solved, were there time enough, by *laissez-faire*, by leaving wages to the free play of the market and the price mechanism. As Sismondi pointed out a century ago, the arguments of *laissez-faire* are perfectly logical and everything works out to an equilibrium in the long run. But, as he asked a hundred years before Keynes asked it again, have we got a long run? And certainly we must ask whether we have got such a long run to-day. Is there the slightest chance that we should be given time to settle these problems by *laissez-faire*? Therefore the only practical policy is the third policy, that is, to say to the whole of industry, "If you object to allowing industry to be co-ordinated with industry by the all-powerful Government, then you must co-ordinate them yourself. First you must equip yourselves with the machinery of co-ordination."

The ambition of the Trade Unions to prevent wages from becoming a matter of detailed Government regulation is a laudable one. The condition of its achievement is that each industry pays adequate attention to the needs of all other industries in deciding its wages, and it must have the machinery that will enable it to do so.

Therefore it is essential that above the Whitley Councils of the particular industries there should be a general House of Industry at large—a third Chamber of Parliament, to which members shall be elected by those engaged in industry, voting in occupational rather than in geographical constituencies. At present it is a common complaint that some Parliamentary constituencies are not properly represented because their members are in reality nominees of their Trade Unions rather than members for the constituency. There are other members who are more concerned to represent some other business interests than to represent their constituencies. Bagehot in his day spoke of "the two hundred members for the railways". It would be much more healthy if such persons, whose prime interests are in the purely industrial rather than in general problems, could find their spiritual homes in a confessedly Industrial

Chamber and could leave the political Parliament to genuine representatives. The details of the methods of election are fair matters for debate, but it is essential that the members of this House be directly elected and not merely nominated by the Trade Unions and the parallel governing bodies of the employers, nor, as in Mr. Churchill's Romanes scheme, elected by the political Parliament.

In this country the project of a House of Industry, as has been said, traces itself back to the first schemes of reconstruction after the 1914 war. In the debate on the Address in February 1919, suggestions were made which led to the setting up of the National Industrial Conference and to the project for a permanent National Industrial Council of four hundred, two hundred representing the employers' organizations and two hundred representing the Trade Unions. According to the argument of this book it was probably a mistake to make the members representatives of the organizations of the two sides of industry. The phrase itself is a bad phrase. It is untrue that industry is rigidly divided into two classes—masters and men—and it is a fault in any constitutional machinery if it seeks so to divide them. Again, we should always be suspicious of people who claim to speak for other people. It is from them that most of our troubles have come. "No man", said William Morris, "is good enough to be another man's master." In any event that plan was dropped from the programme of Mr. Lloyd George's Government in the general reaction against all constructive policy which followed on the slump of 1920.

However, at about the same time a similar idea was put forward from the Socialist side in Mr. and Mrs. Sidney Webb's *Constitution for a Socialist Commonwealth of Great Britain*. In that book the absurdities of attempting to carry out a Socialist revolution with the existing Parliamentary machinery—absurdities of which our own times have given only too telling an example—are cogently exposed. Their suggestion is the establishment of two separate co-equal Parliaments—a Political Parliament responsible for external affairs, defence and justice, and a Social Parliament working largely through committees and responsible for industrial policy. In 1930 Mr. Churchill in his Romanes Lecture advocated the establishment of a House of Industry, possessed of functions not dissimilar to those of the Webbs' Parliament, but definitely subordinate to the political and traditional Parliament. The whole case has been brilliantly and cogently restated by Mr. Amery in his *Thoughts on the Constitution* in our own times. Mr. Harold Macmillan advocated it in a speech at Brighton on March 5, 1949.

Arguments of prejudice can easily be brought forward against such schemes. For instance, when I have argued with friends in the Transport and General Workers' Union in favour of the introduction of a more generous measure of election into their governing affairs, I have often received the answer, "Oh, that is what the Communists advocate." It is thought that this is a final answer. But the Trade Union world is often guilty of exactly the same mistake as that made by Lord Liverpool and Lord Castlereagh immediately after 1815. Then there was fear of Jacobin revolution and every reform, however, moderate, was opposed, on the ground that that was what the Jacobins were advocating and that to grant it was to play into their hands. The effect was exactly the opposite. The effect was to make a present to the revolutionaries of a large number of reasonable arguments, which they could not otherwise have claimed exclusively for their own, and Canning and Huskisson, when they came to power after Castlereagh's suicide, saw clearly that such a policy, far from making revolution impossible, was likely rather to make it inevitable. They reversed the policy and thus compelled the revolutionaries either to go out of business or else to move over to extreme arguments which revealed them in their true colours. So in the same way it is a fatal mistake of the moderate trade-unionists to-day to refuse a sensible reform just because the Communists demand it. Such tactics play into the Communists' hands and present them wantonly with effective battle-cries.

Others attack plans for a House of Industry from the

opposite side and say, "This is the Corporative State. This is Fascism." If it is foolish to reject good ideas just because they have been sponsored by Communists, it is equally foolish to reject good ideas just because they have been sponsored by Fascists. They should be judged on their own merits. There was nothing wrong with the idea of a Parliament of Industry in Fascist Italy. What was wrong was the Fascist control of elections which prevented the Italian workers from a genuine representation and the Government control of the freedom of that Parliament. The Camera Corporativa in Portugal has worked well, and, if, as is doubtless the case, the Portuguese Government has its faults, they are irrelevant to this argument. In the new French constitution there is a functional advisory Chamber, and so far that has been the least criticized part of that constitution.

In the full corporative State the industrial Parliament would be substituted for the political-geographical Parliament. That would indeed be a most grave breach with tradition and one which we are not concerned to advocate. Important as our industrial life is, we should be sorry to be guilty of the heresy of saying that it was the whole of our life and that all our problems could be solved in terms of industry. The solution of the Webbs'—the establishment of two completely independent Parliaments—is in the absolute form in which they proposed it clearly not practical politics. Hardly a day passes but we are reminded, with patent truth, by Mr. Bevin that he could pursue a much more effective foreign policy if only the nation had some coal to export. It is obvious that foreign policy and industrial policy are most intimately connected, and to entrust the two to two utterly unco-ordinated, co-equal authorities, independent of one another, is quite unrealistic.

On the other hand, it is essential that this new House of Industry be more than a debating society and that it be given a definite share in legislative responsibilities. Without such responsibilities it cannot in any way lighten the burden on the traditional Parliament.

The model for it is the Assembly of the Church of England. From the Reformation until recent years the only legislative authority for the Church of England was Parliament. Quite apart from the abstract question of the proper relation between Church and State, this was perhaps a defensible arrangement in the sixteenth or seventeenth centuries when theory still asserted that all Englishmen were members of the Church of England and when there was a general interest in theological problems. By modern times, when only a proportion of members of Parliament belonged to the Church of England, and when, owing to the general growth of ignorance, theological knowledge was confined to a few, the arrangement was frankly absurd and almost blasphemous. Theological questions of high moment and technicality were submitted to a Parliament, of which only a handful of members had the smallest qualification for expressing an opinion. The arrangement was about as sensible as if we were to decide whether an invalid should undergo an operation by universal suffrage, in which the vote of the surgeon counted only as a single vote. Therefore it was decided by the Enabling Act that the Church Assembly should have the right to legislate on the Church's affairs, but, since it was thought that so long as the Church claimed the prestige of a State Church, the State had a right to exercise at least a general and over-riding control over its policy, it was decided that any legislation passed by the Church Assembly must lie on the table of the House for a time, during which the House could, if it wished, annul it. If not annulled during the appropriate period, it then receives the force of law.[1]

Apply a similar solution to industry. At present the processes of industrial legislation are almost insane in their illogicality. The only sort of question on which the electorate in any way pronounces an opinion is the entirely general question, "Are you in favour of the nationalization of (say)

[1] Mr. Walpole in his most valuable *Management and Men* gets this point oddly wrong. He thinks that the Assembly has a veto on Parliament. It is, of course, Parliament which has a veto on the Assembly.

the mines?" Yet nationalization is but a word and the answer largely turns on the particular scheme of nationalization. Now on a particular scheme there are clearly three degrees of opinion, which it is important to discover. First, we wish to know what the workers in the industry think— the actual miners, the actual managers, the actual working owners. (Their opinion is far more important than that of officials of the National Union of Mineworkers or of the Coal Owners' Association, who may or may not misrepresent their constituents). Secondly, we wish to know the opinions of industry at large, since it is obviously a major interest to industry that the supply of coal should be cheap and plentiful. Thirdly, the ordinary citizen, speaking through his representatives in Parliament, has a right to express his opinion, since behind all technical questions there always stand the general metaphysical questions what sort of society and what sort of life we wish to have.

Now, if we take the example of the nationalization of the mines, we can see that that question was handled about as badly as it could have been handled. Obviously the miners, for better or for worse, were in favour of the nationalization of the mines, and, therefore, when they were presented with a Bill for nationalization and with no alternative but to accept it or reject it, they accepted it sooner than play into the hands of their traditional enemies, the coal-owners and the Conservative party. But that does not mean that they liked the plan or that Mr. Shinwell's nationalization bore any more than a nominal resemblance to the nationalization which had been preached to them for a generation. In the Bill introduced by Mr. George Hall (as he then was) in 1923, the Government of the mines was to be vested in a board consisting of ten nominees of the Government and ten representatives of the miners, and a considerable measure of decentralization was to be introduced. In Mr. Shinwell's scheme there was no mention of the miners from beginning to end and the industry was cursed with an over-centralized machinery which made the running of the industry quite impossible and the disorder which followed the attempt to run it quite inevitable.

Now there are in fact two separate issues raised by the mines or by any of our other industries. First, there is the issue of principle. Shall the mines be nationalized? Let that question be settled by the community through its representatives in Parliament. But, once that question is answered in the affirmative, then follows the totally different question: What scheme of nationalization is the most likely to work? That is not an ideological but a technical question. On it the opinion of the man-in-the-street, and indeed the opinion of the average member of Parliament, is worth very little. Yet, according to our constitution, as it is now, Parliament is the only body that has any opportunity of expressing an opinion on such a scheme. In the House of Commons the vast majority of the members, whether on the one side or the other, were not competent to express an opinion. There were a number of mining members, who were perfectly competent to express an opinion and who were well aware that the scheme could not possibly work but who were prevented from saying so by party loyalty. As a result, practical and informed criticism of the Bill was left to those few members outside the Trade Union ranks, such as Colonel Lancaster, who chanced both to be members of the House of Commons and also to have first-hand experience of the mining industry. They were, needless to say, but a tiny handful and their voting strength in opposition to the lobby-fodder that trooped through the lobbies ignorant almost of the elements of the question on which it was voting, was negligible.

We complain—and rightly complain—that Bills of the first moment are remitted to Standing Committees upstairs. Yet it would be no remedy to take all those Bills on the floor of the House—except indeed in so far as it would be a remedy that fewer Bills in all should be passed. We have perhaps forgotten, in our righteous concern at the growth of Standing Committees, how absurd a business the consideration of technical Bills by a Committee of the whole House was in the old days found to be. "One of the most hopeless exhibitions", Bagehot told us eighty years ago, "of helpless ingenuity and wasted mind is a Committee of the whole House on a Bill of many clauses, which eager enemies are trying to spoil and various friends are trying to mend."

The problem can only be solved through a House of Industry. That House would in its turn have Committees of the various particular industries, similar to the Foreign Affairs, the Naval, Military and other Committees of the American Congress or the French Parliament. These committees, largely corresponding to the present Whitley Councils, would consist of the members of that House elected by the industry in question. Whenever a measure was proposed for the reorganization of a particular industry, this measure would be submitted in the first instance to the relevant committee. They would report on it to the House of Industry. It would be reasonable that the House should pay great attention to a Committee's report, but it would not be bound by its recommendation. For there is always a possibility that a particular industry will attempt to hold the community to ransom, and it is necessary to guard against the extremes of syndicalism. Undesirable as it would be in itself, it might on occasions be necessary for industry as a whole to refuse the demands of some particular industry, or even perhaps to force on an industry a scheme which it disliked.

On the other hand, it is much more difficult to conceive circumstances under which it would be wise to force on industry at large a policy of which industry at large disapproved. Therefore the functions of the particular committees should be advisory, but the functions of the House of Industry should have a semi-legislative force. The House of Industry should play in industrial affairs the part which the Church Assembly plays in ecclesiastical affairs. Legislation on the technical details of industrial matters should in the first instance be passed by it. It would then be laid on the table of the political House of Commons, who would have the power to reject it within a given time. If they did

not challenge it within that time, then it would automatically become law. In practice it would be hoped that,
as in ecclesiastical matters, the House of Commons would
not challenge detailed technical legislation, being satisfied
that it had been properly considered by qualified persons in
an atmosphere as little partisan as possible, but on the other
hand would very properly demand its right to a full debate
and to an "Aye" or "No" whenever a matter of large
principle was raised.

It may be objected that this House of Industry would be
at perpetual deadlock owing to the conflict of interest
between those venerable and tiresome myths, "the two sides
of industry". If it got off to a bad start and its affairs were
mishandled, this might happen. It is a risk. But, so long
as it kept to the practical issues which demand a solution
whatever the form of the organization of industry, I do not
myself believe that that would happen. I believe that those
who think that it would happen, from whichever side they
come, are persons who still live in the old pre-war atmosphere
of the conflict between labour and capital—an atmosphere
that is now irrelevant and whose slogans no longer have
any meaning. It was notable that, when the Government
issued its White Paper on the economic state of the nation
at the beginning of 1947, the constructive criticisms on it
of the Trade Union Congress and of the Federation of
British Industries were almost identical. I believe that on
the contrary there are to-day many people in responsible
positions of every sort in industry who rightly do not want a
National Government but who at the same time dislike
the atmosphere of party politics for themselves, and who
would jump at a chance to work in an atmosphere where
they could forget party politics without being called upon
to deny their loyalties. Set them to a practical problem
which cannot be solved by ideological slogans, and there
was never a time when the differences between responsible
leaders of what are known as labour and capital were as
small as they are to-day. Differences will doubtless reveal
themselves, and ought to reveal themselves in the House of

Industry, but I do not believe that the line of difference will run crudely along the line of labour and capital.

Relieved of the details of industrial legislation, for which it is manifestly incompetent, the political and traditional Parliament will find its programme one to which it can pay proper attention and by paying proper attention to it, it will be able to regain that prestige in the eyes of the nation which it has at present so sadly lost. There is no reason why with the lightened programme most, if not all, of the checks on Parliamentary freedom should not be abolished. Private members time could be restored. Legislation by delegation could be reduced to a minimum. The reference of a Bill to a Standing Committee could either be abolished or confined to such Bills as aroused no general interest in the House. The guillotine and closure could be reserved as weapons to be used only against genuine and deliberate obstruction. In fact and in a phrase, Parliamentary government, which is at present in abeyance, could be restored.

Chapter X

LIBERTY IN THE NEW WORLD

THERE ARE in all schools of thought some among those who propound solutions of our industrial and constitutional problems of whom it can fairly be said that they write as if Britain were some utopian island, separated from all the rest of civilization and as if we could do what we ideally thought best, indifferent to the world around us. Alas, it is far from so. In the nineteenth century Britain had almost a manufacturing monopoly. There was no way of coming to this island except by sea, and we had the command of the sea. Our population was rapidly multiplying. We could, to an extent that no other country has ever been able before or since, adopt the solutions which happened to please us. To-day we are most narrowly bound to the conditions of survival. We must do not what we would absolutely like best to do but the best that is possible in such a world as this.[1]

We have irrevocably lost our manufacturing monopoly, we are far from being self-supporting. It is of vital importance that we greatly increase our home production of food—

---

[1] Whether the moralist likes it or not, the economist and the statesman can never afford to forget Veblen's Theory of Conspicuous Waste. Veblen reminds us that, once they rise above subsistence level, people spend the greater part of their incomes on vanity—not on things that they really want for their own sakes but on things that will bring them consideration from their neighbours, in fact on "keeping up with the Joneses". This may be deplorable. It may (or may not) be possible to do something about it on the home market. It is clearly not possible to do anything about it on an export market. International insecurity is to-day causing, and will increasingly cause, nations to make themselves as far as possible self-supporting in necessities. In any event we have little in the way of essential raw materials to export. Therefore our export trade is bound to be predominantly in luxuries and quality goods, and, if we must "export or die", it follows that our luxury trades are to us more important than our trade in necessities. Also it is manifestly true that you cannot hope for a flourishing export trade from an industry that is not allowed to experiment on its home market. Therefore for this country an extreme of "economic puritanism" is not a possible policy.

and we can increase it greatly. Yet however much our production of food may be increased, we shall still need large imports if we are to survive, and now that our foreign investments have so largely gone, we can only import if we can export. Therefore all our debates about standards of living, social services, industrial organization must inevitably be conducted under the constant knowledge that we can only live, if we can sell abroad, and that we can only sell abroad if we put goods on foreign markets of the kind that foreigners want and at prices which they are prepared to pay.

There is a strange paradox in the modern English mind. It is thought a great sign of moral inferiority that an individual should have a higher standard of living than his neighbour but a great sign of moral superiority that a nation should have such a higher standard than another nation. The English dustman thinks it wicked that the English duke should be richer than he is but he does not think it wicked that he himself should be richer than the Chinese dustman. On the contrary, it is a mark of the superiority of the English that his standard of living should be higher than that of the Chinese, and it is this assumption of superiority which to the foreigner makes all denunciation of privilege in British mouths appear ridiculous, since to the foreigner the great privilege is to be British at all. We can preserve the privileges of that status if we can continue to render to the rest of the world services which the world wishes to receive—but we cannot preserve it otherwise. We have no divine right to be kept by the world at our privileged status for no reason at all.

There is a second way in which the whole pattern of international trade is to-day changed. In the early years of the Industrial Revolution Great Britain, then the only industrialized country, exported more than she imported. She did so by exporting on loan through making foreign investments. But Great Britain also adopted free trade and, as a consequence, her debtors could pay her in any goods that they could sell on her markets. As she was a small country, possessed of none of the important raw materials of manufacture except coal and iron, every increase in her exports automatically caused a certain increase in imports—in the imports of raw materials for the new manufactures. As a result there was never any vast unbalance between British exports and imports, and from the middle of the nineteenth century, though we still continued to invest abroad, yet, allowing for the goods imported in payment of dividends on foreign investments and other invisibles, the balance of visible trade was unfavourable to us. Each year we imported more than we exported.

The United States has to-day succeeded to us as the leading industrial country in the world. But, whereas we were a free trade country, the United States is a highly protectionist country. Whereas we are a small country possessed only of a limited number of raw materials, the United States is a large country possessed of almost every raw material which she needs for her industry. Therefore the capture of a new export market by the United States does not automatically bring an increase in imports, as did the capture of a new export market by Great Britain in the nineteenth century.

As a result, ever since the United States became a great creditor country in the 1914 war she has had a vast surplus of exports over imports. The demand of Americans to be paid their debts while at the same time they were virtually refusing to be paid them by their exclusion of their debtors' goods, the sudden realization by the American investor that here was a system under which he could never be repaid, the consequent panic withdrawal of American foreign credits were the main causes of the world's dislocation in the years between the wars. Now it is, of course, perfectly true to-day that with the terrible impoverishment of the rest of the world other countries desperately need American goods and could not immediately pay for them whatever might be the tariff arrangements of America. Yet it is enormously dangerous if people should argue as if the American surplus of exports was some temporary phenomenon of a year or two, caused by the dislocations of war and likely to be cured as soon as other countries are, as the phrase goes, "put on their feet again". It is asking for catastrophe if other countries assume debtor obligations to America—obligations which can only be fulfilled if the world has a favourable balance of trade with America—a balance which there is not the remotest prospect of its achieving within measurable time. Without such a balance the only effect of a recovery of America's debtors must necessarily be a cut-throat competition between them to force their goods on to the American market, and the very return of prosperity must of itself necessarily bring catastrophe.

The basic fact is clear. America does to-day export and will in the future continue to export vastly more than she imports. She is anxious to do this for reasons larger than reasons of business in the narrow sense. She is anxious to do this because of her generosity she does not wish to see other people starve, because of her wisdom she does not wish to see them fall victims to Communism, because of her foresight she understands that if she made too large the gap between the American standard of living and the standards of the rest of the world she would inevitably create world-wide hostility to her that would be to her disadvantage in the long run. All these anxieties are enormously to her credit, but they do not alter the fact that, so long as her exports exceed her imports, she cannot be paid debts in the long run, and, if she cannot be paid debts in the long run, it would be much better both in her own interests and in those of the world that she should make up her mind to it that she cannot be paid then in the short run— that she devise a method of sending goods abroad without putting foreigners into her debt.

During the war Mr. Herbert Feis, a distinguished official of the American Treasury, put forward in the review *Foreign Affairs*, a plan by which America's post-war trade should be conducted. According to that plan a Clearing House should be established in New York. Any American who sold an article to, say, a Frenchman, would receive payment for that article in dollars from the New York

Clearing House. Thus the individual American manufacturer would be taken care of. At the same time the French buyer would pay into the Clearing House the purchase price in francs. A time-limit of, say, seven years would be fixed. If during those seven years any American wished to buy French goods he could obtain the francs from the Clearing House in exchange for dollars, but, if at the end of the seven years the francs had not been used, then they would be cancelled. They would not be allowed to pile up indefinitely as irrepayable debt to bedevil international economic arrangements. If during the seven years Americans should not want French goods but should want the goods of some other country in excess of their holdings of that country's money, then there is no reason why the Clearing House should not convert the francs into the desired currency provided that it could find a purchaser, as it would presumably be able to do unless the French economy was totally out of balance not only with America but with all of the rest of the world.

Who could lose out of such an arrangement? The American exporter could not lose, because he would be immediately paid in dollars. The American importer could not lose, because whenever he wanted foreign goods he could get them. The rest of the world could not lose because it would get all the American goods with which the Americans saw fit to supply it. The whole world would be immeasurably the gainer as it would be saved from the recurrent dislocations caused by the attempt to work a debt system under conditions in which it is mathematically impossible that it should work. The present absurdity by which desperately impoverished nations expend their energies in trying to force on an American market which does not want them the goods which they themselves can ill spare could be ended forever.

The only loser, it may be said, would be the American taxpayer, the general American public, which would be consuming less than it produced and giving away goods to the rest of the world. This is, of course, true and it fully

justifies the Americans in taking all measures to see to it
that they are only providing the rest of the world with the
goods that it really needs, but America has decided that it is
in her interest and the interest of the world that she should
make the world these gifts anyway. All that the Feis Plan
does is to provide a way by which she can do this without
dislocating the economy of the world.

There is no doubt that America will eventually come to
adopt the Feis Plan or something of that nature. Step by
step, over the last twenty years the new economics have
established themselves. Every step in their progress has been
at first denounced by the orthodox as insane, wild, utopian,
impractical and then eventually adopted by the orthodox
as something that they themselves have believed in all
along, and there is no doubt that the same fate awaits the
Feis Plan. But this is the Americans' business. It is for the
converts among them to convert their fellow countrymen.
It is beyond question true that the Americans will themselves
be richer if they give away a large number of goods to the
rest of the world. But though true, it is a strange paradox.
We are not entitled to complain if it takes the American
electorate a. little time to grasp it. People in Europe are
perhaps still a little too complacent about the quantity of
goods which America has to spare. It has yet to be seen
whether the Americans have not permanently damaged
the fertility of their soil in their eagerness to grow all the
food they can for a starving Europe, and they are entitled
to demand that they commit themselves only with caution.
Indeed it is extraordinary how far they have moved in two
years and the foreigner is likely to do more harm than good
if he interferes with lectures and seeks to dictate to the
Americans what they should do. The Americans must be
left to work their problem out for themselves.

The practical question of the moment is—What should
be our policy until the Americans adopt the Feis Plan or its
equivalent? We are often told that we must choose between
bilateral and multilateral trade, that, if we discriminate
against other nations, we must expect other nations to

discriminate against us. It is a false and foolish antithesis, even more foolish than the parallel antithesis in domestic policy of the choice between nationalization and free enterprise. Both antitheses, so far from stating the issue fairly, betray a total unconsciousness of what the issue is.

During the nineteenth century we were in the predominant position. We did not discriminate against other nations but nevertheless allowed other nations to discriminate against us. Cobden hoped that other nations would follow us into free trade, but, when they very sensibly did not do so, we did not make it a cause of complaint against them. We did not haul them along to an international conference and make them sign ridiculous instruments of their devotion to free trade and then make those instruments yet more ridiculous by peppering them with escape clauses to say that everybody could impose tariffs whenever he wanted. In economics as in politics there was far more genuine internationalism in the nineteenth century when there were no international organizations than there is in these days of platitude, discord and pompous conferences. We cannot make sense of international trade so long as we pretend that the United States is "a contracting party" of the same kind as any of the other nations of the world. We cannot have free unilateral trade with the Russians and their satellites—but that is not our fault. We can have, and should have, trade as free as possible with the rest of the world—Western Europe and the countries of the Empire, with whom our books are reasonably in balance. A bold and constructive migration policy should distribute the English-speaking population more evenly over the face of the globe. A proper distribution of population is one of the surest foundations of strength. But, so long as there is this complete lack of balance, then it is both in our interest and in America's interest that we and all the rest of the world should discriminate firmly against America—should keep in our hands full power only to take from America such goods as it is not possible for us to get elsewhere. The argument that, if we have freedom to discriminate against America, America must have freedom to discriminate against us, is absurd. If America's exports vastly exceed her imports, then obviously it is in her own interest that she should give away to the world as little as possible. It is in her interest that she should be discriminated against and that she plan the expansion of her industry for the satisfaction of an enlarged home market rather than for further exports. Even if the world only takes from her the goods that it needs the balance of trade in her favour will be formidable enough. If it takes from her all the goods that she sends along, the problem is utterly insoluble and catastrophe inevitable.

The root fault of the Agreements of the Anglo-American Loan and the Geneva Agreements lies not in this or that detail of the bargain between the Powers. It is not the detail but the whole purpose which is at fault. The ambition to get rid of discrimination, to merge Britain and America into a single economic unit is an ambition that must bring inevitable disaster to both countries. The two nations are at wholly different stages of industrial and economic development. America is still in that crude, optimistic, growing stage through which Britain passed in the nineteenth century. Americans with their gambling temperament do not really wish to get rid of the alternation of boom and slump. They prefer the excitement of a life of ups and downs, and think that the nation emerges out of each depression having indeed suffered some casualties but emerges the stronger and the richer for having cut out its dead wood. So it has been in the past. So it may continue to be for some time in the future in America. No one can doubt that the American economy is heading for another depression in some degree, but it may well be that America with her gigantic resources will be able to ride through that depression with tolerable ease. But there is no reason to think that we shall be able to ride through it in our battered condition. What to them would be but a passing ripple would be to us an Atlantic breaker, and it is madness to tie ourselves up as a junior partner to this economy, that is at an utterly different stage to our own.

It is the strangest of all history's paradoxes that this unconditional surrender to American capitalism should have been made by a British Socialist Government. For after all what is Socialism but discrimination and, if a Socialist Government admits that its aim is to "eliminate discrimination", it might as well be frank and admit that its aim is to destroy Socialism. Indeed such clearly is the consequence, whether it be the understood aim or not, of the present Socialist Government. It has affiliated the country to the International Monetary Fund whose declared purpose it is by its articles of incorporation to "encourage private foreign investment". The Socialists may be willing enough to clip the wings of the domestic capitalist, whom they can tax and can control, but they only do so in order to hand us over to the foreign capitalist whom they cannot tax and cannot control.

The best thing that the Socialists have done has been their policy of Empire Development. But what purpose is there in spending capital on Empire Development if at the same time you bind yourself not to increase any existing preferences nor to impose any new preferences? It will simply mean that millions will be spent on developing the production of the Empire and that it will then be impossible to find a market for those products. There is an equal illogic in the American ambition to eliminate preference and discrimination. The Marshall Plan only makes sense on the assumption that it is an American interest that Western Europe and the British Empire should be strong. It is only through union that they can be strong. A rigid interpretation of the "most favoured nation" principle must inevitably make them divided and weak and defeat the whole purpose of the Marshall policy. It is useless to solve our domestic problems if our foreign and Imperial problems remain unsolved.

CHAPTER XI

COMMUNISM AND INDUSTRIAL DEMOCRACY

COMMUNISM, in the sense of the classless society, has no real bearing on the inquiry of this book, for this book is concerned with realities, and there is no prospect at all that the triumph of the Marxians is leading, or would lead, to the establishment of a classless society. It obviously leads to the establishment of a particularly virulent and violent form of class society. But what we are concerned with is not the utopian future in which the State will "wither away" —a future in whose advent there is not the least reason to believe—but the immediate and intermediate stage of the tyranny of dictatorship of the proletariat, which has already established itself over so large a portion of the world and which may well establish itself over much more. We are concerned with the awful coincidence of the existence of this totalitarian tyranny side by side with weapons of destruction appallingly greater than were ever before known to man. The totalitarian tyranny is not for the moment the master of the worst of those weapons. But none can comfort himself that, if no positive policy be pursued, it will not soon be the master both of those weapons and of weapons even more horrible than have at present been conceived.

We have moved into a new world—a world of unspeakably horrible weapons, against which our geography gives us no especial protection, indeed before which, with our small area and concentrated population, we are especially vulnerable. So far from time being on our side, it is the especial menace of the atom bomb that it favours the most tyrannical and the most wholly totalitarian nation. The ruler who has to pay any attention to his public opinion, who has to submit his policy to any sort of constitutional forms, is at a disadvantage that is likely to prove a fatal disadvantage before the irresponsible ruler who can act without a moment's warning. Therefore the very necessities of salvation inevitably dictate that, if these weapons should become a general possession of the nations, all free institutions must necessarily perish both in Great Britain and in all other countries. Already, even before these weapons have become a general possession, we have had the extraordinary spectacle of a Socialist Government in this country introducing conscription in time of peace. What shall we see when the weapons have become a general possession?

The law of this new world will be a law of the Survival of the Unfreest.

Therefore we are faced with this dilemma. The nature of Western Man demands freedom and without freedom he cannot survive. The strategy of the world of the new weapons demands the destruction of all freedom and the society in which any relic of freedom is tolerated must necessarily perish. In such a world Western Man is inevitably doomed— as much for spiritual as for strategic and geographical reasons. That being so, our only chance is to escape from the dilemma by a bold and positive policy while there is still time. While there is still time and before the totalitarians have developed these new weapons, let the free nations make their demands upon them and demand the total abolition of such weapons. Such a demand would probably be accepted to-day. Admittedly there is a risk on making it. But, if it be not made, then destruction is certain.

It is certain, because the Marxian faith, honestly held by its disciples, drives them, willy-nilly, along a road of continuing world conflict. Such a conflict with the weapons of Marx's day the world could have sustained, for all the inconvenience that it would have brought. But continuing conflict in a world of the atomic bomb and of bacteriological warfare cannot be sustained. It will mean first the destruction of Western Man and in the end in the most literal, physical sense the destruction of the world.

Let us fully understand what is happening in the world to-day according to the Marxian conception. The capitalist system, according to Marx, must inevitably collapse, and must inevitably collapse in violence. "You will have", said Marx to the workers,[1] "to go through fifteen, twenty or fifty years of civil wars and international conflicts, not only to change existing conditions but also to change yourselves and to make yourselves capable of wielding political power." "The working-class", says the communist Manifesto, "cannot simply lay hold of the ready made state machine and wield it for its own purposes." It must first "smash" the old machine.

It is true that as late as 1871 Marx used words in his letter to Kugelmann which are capable of the interpretation that a peaceful transition to Socialism is possible, if not on the continent, at least in England and America. But Stalin in his *Foundations of Leninism* is at pains to point out that, though this may have been possible in the 1870's, subsequent developments have made it impossible. "Marx", writes Stalin, "did in fact concede that possibility, and he had good grounds for conceding it in regard to England and America in the seventies of the last century, when monopoly capitalism and imperialism did not yet exist and when these countries, owing to the special conditions of their development, had as yet no developed militarism and bureaucracy. That was the situation before the appearance of developed imperialism. But later, after a lapse of thirty or forty years, when the situation in these countries had radically changed, when imperialism had developed and had embraced all capitalist countries without exception, when militarism and bureaucracy had appeared in England and America also, when the special conditions for peaceful development in England and the United States had disappeared—then the qualification in regard to these countries necessarily could no longer hold good."

On the contrary, "we are living", Lenin tells us, "not merely in a State, but in a system of States, and the existence of the Soviet Republic side by side with imperialist States for a long time is unthinkable. One or the other must triumph in the end. And before that end supervenes a

[1] Marx, Address to the Workers. Quoted by Lenin, *Selected Works*, vol. 10, p. 151, and by Stalin, *Foundations of Leninism*, p. 41.

series of frightful collisions between the Soviet Republic
and the bourgeois States will be inevitable."[1]   "International imperialism", he said again, "with the entire might
of its capital, with its highly organized military technique,
which is a real force, could not under any circumstances,
on any conditions, live side by side with the Soviet Republic,
both because of its objective position and because of the
economic interest of the capitalist class which are embodied
in it—it could not do so because of commercial connections,
of international financial relations. In this sphere a conflict
is inevitable."[2]   "It would not matter a jot", he thought,
"if three-quarters of the human race perished; the important
thing was that the remaining quarter should be Communists."[3]

Stalin explicitly endorses and quotes both Marx and
Lenin. "The dictatorship of the proletariat", Stalin writes,
"the transition from capitalism to Communism, must not be
regarded as a fleeting period of 'super-revolutionary'
acts and decrees but as an entire historical era, replete with
civil wars and external conflicts."[4]   "The dictatorship of
the proletariat", he writes again, "cannot arise as the result
of the peaceful development of bourgeois society and of
bourgeois democracy; it can arise only as the result of the
smashing of the bourgeois State machine, the bourgeois
army, the bourgeois democratic machine, the bourgeois
police."[5]

That being so, it is of course entirely logical in the Bolsheviks that they have always reserved their major hostility
and their major contempt for Parliamentary Socialists,
who preach and believe that the transformation to Socialism
can be made peacefully and constitutionally. The notion
that Parliamentary Socialism can be a bulwark against
Communism is a fantasy so foolish as to be hardly worth

[1] Lenin, *Selected Works*, Vol. 8, p. 33, quoted by Stalin, *Problems of Leninism*,
p. 160.
[2] Lenin, *Selected Works*. Vol. 7, p. 288
[3] Fülöp-Miller, *Mind and Face of Bolshevism*, p. 85.
[4] Stalin *Foundations of Leninism*, p. 41
[5] Stalin, *Foundations of Leninism*, p 44.

discussing. The value of Parliamentary Socialists in the Communist conception is that they can be used as a stop-gap Government in order to prepare the way for a Communist seizure of power for which public opinion is not yet quite prepared. The Bolsheviks in Russia did not come to power by overthrowing the Czar; they came to power by over-throwing the Parliamentary Socialists. They have always and in every country from Russia to Czechoslovakia come to power by overthrowing the Parliamentary Socialists.

Thus it is perfectly logical in Stalin to write: "Hence the necessity of a stubborn, continuous and determined struggle against the imperialist chauvinism of the 'Socialists' of the ruling nations (Great Britain, France, America, Italy, Japan, etc.) who do not want to fight their imperialist Governments, who do not want to support the struggle of the oppressed in 'their' colonies for emancipation from oppression for secession."[1]   Or, again, "the upper stratum of the proletariat, principally Trade Union leaders and Labour Members of Parliament who are fed by the bourgeoisie out of the super-profits extracted from the colonies, is undergoing a process of decay."[2] "This stratum of bour-geoisified workers of the 'labour aristrocracy'", says Lenin,[3] "who are quite philistine in their mode of life, in the size of their earnings and in their outlook, serves as the principal social (not military) prop of the bourgeoisie. They are the real agents of the bourgeoisie in the Labour movement, the Labour lieutenants of the capitalist class, real channels of reformism and chauvinism."

The Foundations of Leninism indeed shows a marked contrast between its contemptuous references to Parliamentary Socialists and its respectful references to what Stalin calls "American efficiency". Stalin writes,[4] "American efficiency is that indomitable force which neither knows nor recognizes obstacles; which continues at a task once started until it is finished, even if it is a minor task; and without which serious

[1] Stalin, *Foundation of Leninism*, p. 65.
[2] Stalin, *Foundation of Leninism*, p. 90.
[3] Lenin, *Selected Works*, Vol. 5, p. 12.
[4] *Foundations of Leninism*, p. 93

constructive work is inconceivable. . . . The combination of
the Russian revolutionary sweep with American efficiency is
the essence of Leninism in party and State work." This is
because, although it is the Marxian belief that the American,
like all non-Communist societies, is destined for eventual
collapse, yet according to that belief there is such a thing
as "a revolutionary situation". When a nation has installed
a Parliamentary Socialist Government in power, that is
evidence that a revolutionary situation exists and all energy
must be devoted to nursing that situation so that at the
appropriate moment constitutional Socialism can be transformed into revolutionary Socialism. But when the right-
wing Government is effectively in power, that is proof, in
Marxian eyes, that a revolutionary situation does not yet
exist. They are therefore much more willing to treat their
relations with such a Government realistically and on their
intrinsic merits—to trade with them, where trade is to their
immediate advantage, to learn from them such technical
lessons as it may be profitable to learn.

In Marx, as in his great contemporary Wordsworth,
"two voices are there". Marx, the prophet, was a ranter and
a revolutionary, but there was also Marx, the economist and
thinker, who was essentially a conservative or at least an
evolutionary, ready even in the Communist Manifesto
itself, to pay full tribute to the inevitability of capitalism
in its day and place and to the enormous services which it
had rendered to mankind. In his ranting passages, as
Professor Schumpeter writes, in *Capitalism, Socialism and
Democracy*, "Marx himself contradicts his deepest and most
mature thought which speaks out unmistakably from the
analytical structure of *Das Kapital* and—as any thought must
that is inspired by a sense of the inherent logic of things—
carries beneath the fantastic glitter of dubious gems, a
distinctly conservative implication. . . . To say that Marx,
stripped of phrases, admits of interpretation in a conservative sense is only saying that he can be taken seriously."

The Western world can never make terms with Marxianism. Marxianism is an aggressive and militant creed, and

we can only meet a weapon with a weapon. If we would have peace, we must be strong. But we must also meet an idea with an idea. We must also confront the Marxian idea of slavery with the Western idea of freedom. But— hardest task perhaps of all—we must induce the Marxians to read their Marx—induce them to distinguish between the analytical argument for the ephemeral life of capitalism, as Marx knew capitalism, and the apocalyptic and unreasoned rant which screams so wantonly and improbably that Socialism will be its successor—between the demonstration that change must be gradual and the assertion that it must be violent.[1] Of course capitalism cannot be transformed peaceably into the lesser freedom of the Socialist state. That is the very reason why Socialism can never be capitalism's successor. But it can be transformed peaceably into the greater freedom of a distributist philosophy.

---

[1] I do not wish to be guilty of the paradox that all truth is contained in Marx, but at least enough truth is contained in him to refute Marxianism.

CHAPTER XII

THE OPPORTUNITY

I WAS re-reading the other day Maurice Baring's *Puppet Show of Memory*. He tells there how in his young student days in Germany he heard an old professor lecturing. It was the professor's theme that each of the great nations had some especial gift to bring to the world. The Greeks brought art, and the Romans law. " 'England's gift to the world', he said, 'was Freedom', and as he said the word *'Freiheit'*," comments Baring, "his voice rang and we felt all of a tremble."

This is indeed so. The Socialists are, of course, entirely right to jeer at those who identify freedom with the particular form of economic organization known as *laissez-faire*, and their jeers would be even more convincing if it was clear at what responsible person they were directed. "The old order changeth, yielding place to new." One phase of economic arrangement succeeds to another and one form of freedom to another. In each phase, if it is to survive and perform worthily its passing duty of ministering to the strength of England, a place must be found for freedom—a means must be found by which men and women can feel that they are doing that which they judge important in their lives by their own choice and not by external compulsion. From age to age the incidence of freedom changes. In one age men and women value most keenly the right to assert themselves in one direction, in another age in another. In one age it is one element in the State which has attained to inordinate power, in another it is another—now it is the kings, now the landlords, now the capitalists, now the bureaucrats, now the managers. It is the problem of politics in each age to diagnose correctly the disease of that age and to apply the remedy. Only the reactionaries clamour for the liberties of yesterday and only those who have sold them-

selves to despair abandon the whole cause of liberty because
the liberties of yesterday are to-day in some ways irrelevant.

We stand to-day in most desperate peril—peril more
desperate than any in our history. New inventions and new
developments have robbed us of those geographical
advantages through the use of which English freedom has
been able to grow and to endure through the ages. English
freedom can no longer survive as an especial thing, as a
refuge from the tyranny of "less happier lands". It is true
to-day of the world, as it was true of the American nation
in the days of Abraham Lincoln that it cannot endure half
slave and half free. Either it must go forward to a total
freedom or resign itself to a total slavery. These weapons
of sudden destruction must be totally abolished or all
freedom must be totally abandoned.

The obstacles are indeed formidable. It is no time for
complacent prophesying. Yet there is no reason for despair.
The forces in favour of freedom both in the world at large
and in men and women of good will in every party in this
country are overwhelming. All that are needed for victory
are those two most rare things—courage and clear thinking.
It is while men dispute upon irrelevant and outworn issues
that the battle is lost, and that is the luxury of folly that we
cannot afford to-day. We are at least delivered from the
dreariest and most idiotic of all slaveries—the belief in an
automatic and inevitable progress. Salvation is still possible,
but only possible if we have the courage to act in time. A
policy of inaction must inevitably mean disaster.

The development of science and the development of
other nations have combined to rob Britain of the unique
position which she held in the nineteenth century. That
position can never be regained. Yet even in the nineteenth
century our greatest exports to the world were not coal or
cotton. Our greatest exports were ideas and character.
The world needs the ideas of English freedom and the
leadership of English character to-day not only as badly as,
but enormously more than, it has ever needed them. If we
have the courage to speak a language worthy of our destiny,

then we can give to the world a leadership for which it is
crying out more desperately than it has ever cried and which
it will gladly receive. But, if through cowardice, through
confusion, through indolence, through "craven fears of
being great", we miss our opportunity now, then we miss it
forever. The leadership will pass to other hands and it
can never be reclaimed. "England", as Disraeli said, "can
never begin again." If we go down now, we go down forever,
and, if we lose freedom now, we lose it forever. Our spiritual
heritage and our material standards will alike be forfeit.

There are three main tasks which this generation of
Englishmen has to accomplish if it will live. First, it must
join with the men of good will of other nations in banishing
utterly from the world the new weapons of sudden destruction. Secondly, it must recognize that, with modern developments, Britain alone is no longer an economic unit and must
join with the peoples of the Empire and the peoples of
Europe to form that larger economic unit within which
alone Britain can live. Thirdly, it must recognize that freedom
is the spiritual necessity of Western Man and that this
is the age of Industrial Man. It must therefore find a way
of giving the worker in the industrial system, in which so
many millions of men and women must inevitably live their
lives, a way of freedom and of responsibility. These are the
conditions of liberty and of our survival.